WILLIAMS-SONOMA

Chicken for dinner

WELDON OWEN

Contents

Understanding Poultry

Good cooking begins with good-quality ingredients, so it's important to know how to select the best poultry that you can find. A handful of commonsense tips will make shopping for poultry easy.

Fresh poultry is preferred over frozen for its superior flavor and texture. Look for meaty, plump specimens that are free of bruises or tears. Skin color is not necessarily an indication of quality. A wide variety of chicken parts are available, but it's often more economical to buy whole birds and cut or bone them yourself. You'll find step-by-step instructions for cutting and boning chicken parts starting on page 120.

The terms "organic" and "free range" are not standardized and are subject to different interpretations. Generally, organic poultry is fed a diet of feed grown without the use of pesticides. Free-range poultry has at least limited access to the outdoors. The meat is often firmer in texture and more richly flavored than that of cage-raised birds.

Whole birds should look plump, and their skin should be free of discoloration or feathers. The color of the skin depends on the breed and on the diet. Most poultry skin is naturally white, but some growers feed their chickens marigold petals, for example, which give the skin a yellow tint that appeals to many consumers.

Raw poultry labeled "fresh" has never been chilled below 26°F (–4°C), the temperature at

which flesh freezes solid. Poultry stored at 0°F (–18°C) or less is labeled "frozen" or "previously frozen." No labeling is required for poultry that is held at temperatures between these two extremes. So if unfrozen poultry is important to you, make sure it says "fresh" on the label. Any liquid you see in the package is usually water that was absorbed by the bird when it was chilled during processing.

Poultry with fatty skin, such as chicken and duck, freezes well because the fat keeps the flesh moist when the poultry is later cooked. But thawed lean birds or skinless cuts, such as whole turkeys or boneless chicken breasts, can taste dry when cooked, a result that processors try to counteract by injecting the poultry with salty liquids. These moisturizing agents can alter the flavor of the poultry and the recipe seasoning, especially when poultry is brined. For this reason, avoid packages labeled "self-basting" or "treated with saline solution."

Package labels sometimes announce that no hormones have been used in the raising of chickens, though the USDA has actually outlawed their use. Many markets include a sell-by or use-before date on the poultry label. Regardless of that date, use fresh poultry within two days of purchase.

Flavoring & Seasoning

There are myriad ways to flavor versatile poultry. You can enhance a bird's natural flavor before, during, or after cooking. Seasonings, marinades, brines, glazes, pan sauces, and gravies are all delicious options.

Fat, Salt & Pepper

Salt and pepper bring out the inherent flavor of poultry, and nibbling on golden brown chicken skin seasoned with this timeless pair is a delicious indulgence. One of the most satisfying ways to season roast chicken is simply to rub it with oil or softened butter, and then sprinkle it inside and out with salt and pepper. Many chefs now favor kosher or sea salt for their superior flavor as compared to basic table salt. Whenever possible use freshly ground black pepper.

Spice & Herb Rubs

Coating the outside of poultry with a blend of spices or herbs layers potent flavors on the exterior of the bird. The skin should be previously rubbed with softened butter or oil, which not only helps the spices or herbs adhere, but also moistens the dry seasonings and keeps them from burning. When you're making a rub based on whole spices, briefly toast the spices first in a dry frying pan to release their essential oils.

Under-the-Skin Seasoning

You can massage the skin of poultry, whether whole birds or bone-in breasts, underneath the skin using a savory, spreadable mixture like pesto, tapenade, or compound (flavored)

butter. When the mixture heats, it infuses the flesh with flavor, while the skin protects the seasoning from drying and scorching.

Marinades

Marinating poultry is a popular method for enhancing its flavor. More robustly seasoned marinades will generally take less time to deliver flavor, but watch the clock to avoid over-marinating, which can affect the texture of fresh poultry. Marinate poultry in a nonreactive bowl, such as glass, ceramic, or stainless steel to prevent the formation of off colors or flavors.

Brines

Brining is an old-fashioned technique that is making a welcome comeback. This method is one of the best ways to ensure moist poultry, especially with whole birds. The salt in the brine breaks down some of the proteins in the meat, allowing the meat to absorb the flavored brine, resulting in juicier cooked poultry. You'll need to plan ahead, as brining usually requires several hours to work properly. That said, as with marinades, follow time instructions carefully to ensure the proper texture. Also, take care when seasoning pan sauces made after cooking brined chicken, as they may require less salt.

FLAVORS FOR CHICKEN

Mild chicken marries with a multitude of flavors, from herbs to spices, from sweet to savory. Here are a handful of flavoring ideas, inspired by cuisines from around the world, which will appear in the recipes that follow.

Greek Garlic, oregano, and lemon (see Garlic & Oregano Chicken, page 21)

Chinese Ginger, garlic, and soy (see Soy-Glazed Chicken Breasts, page 56)

Latin Cumin, lime, and chiles (see Chicken Tacos, page 48)

Caribbean Chiles, lime, and allspice (see Jerk Chicken Skewers, page 60)

Southern Italian Tomatoes, red wine, rosemary (see Chicken Cacciatore, page 106)

Provençal Tomatoes, garlic, and black olives (see Chicken with Tomatoes & Olives, page 109)

Spanish Bell peppers, smoked paprika, sherry (see Spanish-Style Braised Chicken, page 110)

Moroccan Green olives, lemon, cumin (see Moroccan-Style Chicken, page 112)

Four related techniques—sautéing, panfrying, deep-frying, and stir-frying—are used to cook various poultry cuts quickly. They all involve oil or butter as the cooking medium, which browns the ingredients, creating crisp crusts over moderately high to

Sautéed & Fried

high heat. A common theme with these techniques is a pan sauce, which brings all the flavors together in harmony. The recipes that follow offer a wide range of dishes suitable for any occasion—from a quick weeknight meal option to a casual meal fit for a family get-together to a special occasion meal for company.

Cuts for Sautéing & Frying

The best cuts for sautéing, panfrying, and stir-frying are boneless cuts, such as chicken breasts. Turkey cutlets and duck breasts are also delicious cooked in the frying pan. Bone-in pieces are suitable for deep-frying, as are thin boneless pieces. Many sautéed and panfried recipes call for pounding poultry pieces to ensure even cooking.

Fats for Sautéing & Frying

For sautéing and panfrying, some recipes use both butter and oil for a sound reason. The butter provides flavor, but it burns at a relatively low heat. The oil can withstand higher heat and allows the butter to be heated to an increased temperature. For deep-frying, choose an oil with a high smoke point, such as peanut or canola.

Crumb & Flour Coatings

Apply flavored bread crumbs or seasoned flour to the outside of poultry pieces before sautéing or frying to protect the flesh from the high heat of the cooking fat. This insulation both seals in the juices and adds another layer of flavor and texture to the dish, achieving a crisp, golden crust when browned in the hot fat.

Tips & Tricks

Testing with Your Senses

Thin, tender pieces of poultry are often difficult to test for doneness using a thermometer. Instead, carefully press on the cooked meat with a fingertip and note the texture. When it is done, poultry should feel firm to the touch. You can also cut into the edge of the chicken piece and look to make sure the meat is opaque throughout with no signs of pink.

Deglazing Pan Drippings

Many sautéed and panfried recipes feature a rich-tasting sauce made from the pan drippings. The first step is to dissolve the browned bits, a process called deglazing. Place the pan over medium-high heat. When the drippings sizzle, add stock or another liquid and bring to a boil. Scrape the bottom and sides of the pan with a wooden spatula to loosen and dissolve the bits.

Pans for the Stove Top

A frying pan with an uncoated surface is the best choice when making a pan sauce because it allows flavorful bits to adhere to the pan bottom after sautéing or panfrying. A nonstick pan will work, too, but won't develop as many browned bits. With the latter, use a plastic whisk or other nonmetal tool to avoid scratching the protective coating as you whisk the ingredients.

The browned bits left in the pan after sautéing chicken breasts should not be wasted. Here, they are dissolved in stock, accented with fresh herbs, and enriched with butter for a delicious pan sauce.

Chicken with Tarragon Pan Sauce

- Sprinkle both sides of the breasts with ½ teaspoon salt and ¼ teaspoon pepper. Place a large frying pan over medium-high heat and add 1 tablespoon of the butter and the oil. Meanwhile, spread the flour in a shallow dish. One at a time, lightly coat the breasts with the flour, shaking off excess, and place in the pan.

- Cook until the undersides are golden brown, about 3 minutes. Turn and reduce the heat to medium. Sauté until the second sides are golden brown and the breasts feel firm when pressed in the center with a fingertip, about 3 minutes longer. Transfer to a warmed platter.

- Place the pan over medium heat and add 1 tablespoon of the butter. When the butter has melted, add the shallot and sauté until softened, about 2 minutes. Stir in the tarragon. Add the stock, raise the heat to high, and bring to a boil, scraping up the browned bits on the pan bottom. Cook until the liquid has reduced by one-fourth, about 2 minutes.

- Return the breasts to the pan, turn once, and cook for 1 minute. Transfer the chicken to the platter. Off the heat, whisk in the remaining 1 tablespoon butter until melted. Taste and adjust the seasonings. Spoon the sauce over the chicken and serve right away.

4 boneless, skinless chicken breast halves, 6 oz (185 g) each, lightly pounded until ½ inch (12 mm) thick

Kosher salt and freshly ground pepper

3 tbsp unsalted butter

1 tbsp canola oil

¼ cup (1½ oz/45 g) all-purpose flour

1 shallot, minced

1 tsp chopped fresh tarragon

1 cup (8 fl oz/250 ml) Chicken Stock (page 138) or low-sodium chicken broth

MAKES 4 SERVINGS

This dish is inspired by piccata, the popular Italian preparation. Piccata gets a fresh tang from lemons, a mild brininess from capers, and richness from homemade chicken stock.

Chicken with Lemon & Capers

● Sprinkle both sides of the chicken breast halves with ½ teaspoon salt and ¼ teaspoon pepper.

● Place a large frying pan over medium-high heat and add 1 tablespoon of the butter and the oil. Meanwhile, spread the flour in a shallow dish. One at a time, lightly coat the breasts with the flour, shaking off excess, and place the coated breasts in the pan.

● Cook until the undersides are golden brown, about 3 minutes. Turn and reduce the heat to medium. Sauté until the second sides are golden brown and the breasts feel firm when pressed in the center with a fingertip, about 3 minutes longer. Transfer to a warmed platter.

● Place the pan over high heat and add the stock, wine, lemon juice, and sliced lemon. Bring to a boil, scraping up the browned bits on the pan bottom. Cook until the liquid has reduced by one-fourth, about 2 minutes. Add the capers.

● Return the breasts to the pan, turn once, and cook for 1 minute. Transfer the breasts to warmed individual plates. Off the heat, whisk the remaining 1 tablespoon butter into the sauce until melted. Taste and adjust the seasonings. Spoon the sauce over the chicken and serve right away.

4 boneless, skinless chicken breast halves, 6 oz (185 g) each, lightly pounded until ½ inch (12 mm) thick

Kosher salt and freshly ground pepper

2 tbsp unsalted butter

1 tbsp canola oil

¼ cup (1½ oz/45 g) all-purpose flour

½ cup (4 fl oz/125 ml) Chicken Stock (page 138) or low-sodium chicken broth

½ cup (4 fl oz/125 ml) dry white wine

3 tbsp fresh lemon juice

1 lemon, thinly sliced

2 tbsp capers, rinsed and drained

MAKES 4 SERVINGS

Mustard is a great, easy way to inject flavor into sautéed chicken. It can either be spread directly onto the meat or whisked into a pan sauce, as in this dish. Use your favorite flavored mustard for variety.

Chicken with Mustard-Shallot Sauce

4 boneless, skinless chicken breast halves, 6 oz (185 g) each, lightly pounded until ½ inch (12 mm) thick

Kosher salt and freshly ground pepper

3 tbsp unsalted butter

1 tbsp canola oil

¼ cup (1½ oz/45 g) all-purpose flour

1 shallot, finely diced

¾ cup (6 fl oz/180 ml) Chicken Stock (page 138) or low-sodium chicken broth

¼ cup (2 fl oz/60 ml) dry white wine

1 tbsp plain or herb-flavored Dijon mustard

MAKES 4 SERVINGS

- Sprinkle both sides of the chicken breast halves with ½ teaspoon salt and ½ teaspoon pepper.

- Place a large frying pan over medium-high heat and add 1 tablespoon of the butter and the 1 tablespoon oil. Meanwhile, spread the flour in a shallow dish. One at a time, lightly coat the breasts in the flour, shaking off excess, and place the coated breasts in the pan.

- Cook until the undersides are golden brown, about 3 minutes. Turn and reduce the heat to medium. Sauté until the second sides are golden brown and the breasts feel firm when pressed in the center with a fingertip, about 3 minutes longer. Transfer to a warmed platter.

- Place the pan over medium heat and add 1 tablespoon of the butter. When the butter has melted, add the shallot and sauté until softened, about 2 minutes. Add the stock and wine, raise the heat to high, and bring to a boil, scraping up the browned bits on the pan bottom. Cook until the liquid is reduced by one-fourth, about 2 minutes. Whisk in the mustard.

- Return the chicken breasts to the pan, turn once, and cook for 1 minute. Transfer the chicken breasts to warmed individual plates. Off the heat, whisk in the remaining 1 tablespoon butter until melted. Taste and adjust the seasonings. Spoon the sauce over the chicken and serve right away.

A golden brown, oregano-flecked crumb coating, redolent of garlic, is reason enough to make these chicken breasts. The crust also protects the meat from the heat of the pan to keep it moist.

Garlic & Oregano Chicken

3 thick slices stale crusty bread, torn into large pieces

2 cloves garlic

4 tsp dried oregano

Kosher salt and freshly ground pepper

4 boneless, skinless chicken breast halves, about 6 oz (185 g) each, lightly pounded until ½ inch (12 mm) thick

½ cup (4 fl oz/125 ml) plus 2 tbsp olive oil

4 lemon wedges

MAKES 4 SERVINGS

● With a food processor running, drop the bread pieces through the feed tube, one at a time, and process into coarse crumbs. Transfer to a large bowl.

● With the food processor running, drop the garlic cloves through the feed tube to chop finely. Stop the processor and add the bread crumbs, oregano, ¼ teaspoon salt, and ¼ teaspoon pepper. Pulse to combine.

● Using a pastry brush, coat the chicken breast halves on both sides with the 2 tablespoons oil. Sprinkle both sides evenly with ½ teaspoon salt and ½ teaspoon pepper. Spread the bread crumb mixture in a wide, shallow dish. One at a time, place the breast halves in the crumbs, covering them completely, and pat lightly to help the crumbs adhere. Transfer the coated breasts to a baking sheet.

● Place a very large frying pan over medium-high heat and add the remaining ½ cup oil. When the oil shimmers, place the breast halves in the pan and cook until the undersides are golden, about 4 minutes. Using a slotted spatula, turn and cook the other sides until golden and the breasts feel firm when pressed in the center, about 4 minutes longer. Transfer to paper towels to drain briefly, turning them once, about 30 seconds, then place on warmed individual plates. Place a lemon wedge on each plate for squeezing and serve right away.

Tender-crisp asparagus is a great partner for the soft texture of chicken breasts in this quick stir-fry. Lemongrass has a tangy flavor and lemony fragrance and is a a wonderful accent.

Chicken & Asparagus Stir-Fry

- Heat a wok or extra-large frying pan over high heat until very hot, about 2 minutes. Add the oil and swirl the wok to coat the bottom and sides. Add the chicken, spread out in a single layer, and cook, undisturbed, for 20–30 seconds. Stirring and tossing vigorously with 2 wooden spatulas, continue to cook the chicken until opaque throughout, about 1 minute. Transfer to a plate.

- Add the ginger, lemongrass, and garlic to the pan and stir-fry until fragrant, about 30 seconds. Add the asparagus and stir-fry until tender-crisp, 2–3 minutes.

- Add the broth and fish sauce to the pan and bring to a simmer. Return the chicken and any juices from the plate to the pan, reduce the heat to medium-low, and simmer until heated through, about 1 minute.

- Divide the stir-fry among warmed individual plates, top with the peanuts, and serve right away.

2 tbsp peanut oil

1½ lb (750 g) boneless, skinless chicken breast halves, cut into thin strips

2 tbsp minced fresh ginger

1 stalk lemongrass, bulb part only, finely chopped

3 cloves garlic, minced

½ lb (250 g) asparagus, cut on the diagonal into 1-inch (2.5-cm) lengths

¾ cup (6 fl oz/180 ml) low-sodium chicken broth

2 tbsp Asian fish sauce

¼ cup (1½ oz/45 g) chopped peanuts

MAKES 4 SERVINGS

After you taste this fresh and easy stir-fry, you will never need to call for take out again. Garlic, ginger, and soy characterize this intensely dark sauce, garnished with roasted peanuts.

Kung Pao Chicken

1 tbsp *each* soy sauce and dry sherry

3 tsp cornstarch

1 lb (500 g) boneless, skinless chicken breasts halves, cut into ½-inch (12-mm) slices

½ cup (4 fl oz/125 ml) low-sodium chicken broth

1 tbsp *each* dark Chinese vinegar and sugar

2 tsp Asian sesame oil

About 2 tbsp peanut oil

1 tbsp minced fresh ginger

4 cloves garlic, minced

Red pepper flakes

3 celery stalks, diced

1 red bell pepper, diced

¾ cup (4 oz/125 g) roasted peanuts

MAKES 4 SERVINGS

● In a bowl, combine the soy sauce, sherry, and 1 teaspoon of the cornstarch. Add the chicken, stir until evenly coated, cover, and let stand for 10 minutes.

● In a small bowl, stir together the broth, vinegar, sugar, sesame oil, and the remaining 2 teaspoons cornstarch.

● Heat a wok or extra-large frying pan over high heat until very hot, about 2 minutes. Add 2 tablespoons peanut oil and swirl the wok to coat the bottom and sides. Add the ginger, garlic, and ¾ teaspoon pepper flakes, or to taste, and stir-fry until fragrant, about 10 seconds. Add the chicken with its marinade, spread it out in a single layer, and cook, undisturbed, for 20–30 seconds. Stirring and tossing vigorously with 2 wooden spatulas, continue to cook the chicken until opaque throughout, about 1 minute. Add a little more oil if needed to prevent sticking.

● Add the celery and bell pepper and stir-fry until tender-crisp, about 2 minutes. Stir the sauce mixture well, then add to the wok. Cook, stirring, until the sauce thickens, a few seconds.

● Divide the stir-fry among warmed individual plates, top with the peanuts, and serve right away.

For this recipe, or for any stir-fry, be sure to have all the components prepared and ready at the stove, as the cooking goes very quickly. Stir-frying is a great option for a quick weeknight meal.

Ginger Chicken & Vegetables

- In a bowl, combine 1 tablespoon of the soy sauce, 1 tablespoon of the sherry, and 1 teaspoon cornstarch. Add the chicken, stir until evenly coated, cover, and let stand for 10 minutes.

- In a small bowl, stir together the broth, the remaining 3 tablespoons soy sauce, the remaining 2 tablespoons of the sherry, the 1 tablespoon cornstarch, and 1/8 teaspoon pepper until the cornstarch is dissolved.

- Heat a wok or extra-large frying pan over high heat until very hot, about 2 minutes. Add 2 tablespoons oil and swirl the wok to coat the bottom and sides well. Add the ginger and stir-fry until fragrant, about 10 seconds. Add the chicken with its marinade, spread it out in a single layer, and cook, undisturbed, for 20–30 seconds. Stirring and tossing vigorously with 2 wooden spatulas, continue to cook the chicken until opaque throughout, about 1 minute. Add a little more oil if the ingredients are sticking.

- Add the mushrooms, stir well, then cover and cook until tender, about 3 minutes. Uncover and stir in the snow peas and green onions. Re-cover and cook until the snow peas are bright green and tender-crisp, about 1 minute.

- Stir the soy sauce mixture well and add to the wok. Cook, stirring, until the sauce thickens, a few seconds. Divide the stir-fry among warmed individual plates and serve right away.

4 tbsp soy sauce

3 tbsp dry sherry

1 tbsp plus 1 tsp cornstarch

1 lb (500 g) boneless, skinless chicken breast halves, cut into 1/2-inch (12-mm) slices

1 1/4 cups (10 fl oz/ 310 ml) low-sodium chicken broth

Freshly ground pepper

About 2 tbsp peanut oil

1 tbsp minced fresh ginger

6 shiitake mushroom caps, cut into 1/4-inch (6-mm) strips

6 oz (185 g) snow peas

4 green onions, cut into 1-inch (2.5-cm) lengths

MAKES 4 SERVINGS

This Italian-inspired sauce is adapted to come together in just minutes on the stove top. Just before serving, you can top the cutlets with sliced mozzarella and broil for a minute until melted.

Turkey Cutlets with Tomato & Basil

- In a very large frying pan over medium heat, heat 1 tablespoon of the oil until it shimmers. Add the shallot and garlic and sauté until the shallot softens, about 2 minutes. Add the tomatoes, basil, vinegar, and pepper flakes. Raise the heat to medium-high, bring to a boil, and cook until the juices thicken, 5–7 minutes. Transfer the tomato sauce to a bowl and wipe clean the pan.

- Sprinkle the cutlets with ½ teaspoon salt and ¼ teaspoon pepper. Place the pan over medium-high heat and add the butter and the remaining 1 tablespoon of the olive oil. Spread the flour in a shallow dish. One at a time, lightly coat the cutlets with the flour, shaking off the excess, and place the coated breasts in the pan.

- Cook until the undersides are golden brown, about 3 minutes. Turn and reduce the heat to medium. Sauté until the second sides are golden brown and the cutlets feel firm when pressed in the center with a fingertip, about 3 minutes longer. Transfer to a warmed platter.

- Return the tomato sauce to the pan and bring to a boil, scraping up the browned bits on the pan bottom. Return the cutlets to the pan, turn once, and cook for 1 minute. Transfer the cutlets to warmed individual plates. Taste the sauce and adjust the seasonings.

- Spoon the tomato sauce over the cutlets and serve right away.

2 tbsp olive oil

1 shallot, minced

1 clove garlic, minced

2 cups (12 oz/375 g) drained and chopped canned tomatoes

2 tbsp chopped fresh basil

1 tbsp red wine vinegar

⅛ tsp red pepper flakes

1¼ lb (625 g) turkey cutlets, lightly pounded until ¼ inch (6 mm) thick

Kosher salt and freshly ground black pepper

1 tbsp unsalted butter

¼ cup (1½ oz/45 g) all-purpose flour

MAKES 4 SERVINGS

For a taste of Thanksgiving without a lot of fuss, a sauce of dried cranberries tops sautéed turkey cutlets. Turkey cutlets are cut from the breast meat and are perfectly suited to quick cooking.

Turkey Cutlets with Cranberries

½ cup (2 oz/60 g) dried cranberries

½ cup (4 fl oz/125 ml) tawny or ruby Port

1¼ lb (625 g) turkey cutlets, lightly pounded until ¼ inch (6 mm) thick

Kosher salt and freshly ground pepper

2 tbsp unsalted butter

1 tbsp olive oil

¼ cup (1½ oz/45 g) all-purpose flour

1 cup (8 fl oz/250 ml) Chicken Stock (page 138) or low-sodium chicken broth

1 tbsp balsamic vinegar

MAKES 4 SERVINGS

● In a small saucepan, combine the dried cranberries and Port and bring to a boil. Turn off the heat and let stand until the cranberries soften, about 30 minutes.

● Sprinkle the cutlets with ½ teaspoon salt and ½ teaspoon pepper.

● Place a very large frying pan over medium-high heat and add 1 tablespoon of the butter and the olive oil. Meanwhile, spread the flour in a shallow dish. One at a time, lightly coat the cutlets with the flour, shaking off the excess, and place the coated breasts in the pan.

● Cook until the undersides are golden brown, about 3 minutes. Turn and reduce the heat to medium. Sauté until the second sides are golden brown and the cutlets feel firm when pressed in the center with a fingertip, about 3 minutes longer. Transfer to a warmed platter.

● Add the cranberries and Port to the pan and bring the liquid to a boil, scraping up the browned bits on the pan bottom. Stir in the stock and vinegar. Cook until the sauce is reduced to about ⅓ cup (3 fl oz/80 ml), about 3 minutes.

● Return the turkey to the pan, turn once, and cook for 1 minute. Transfer the cutlets to warmed individual plates. Off the heat, whisk the remaining 1 tablespoon butter into the sauce until melted. Taste and adjust the seasonings.

● Spoon the cranberry-Port sauce over the cutlets and serve right away.

A soak in buttermilk brine is what makes this fried chicken, with its spicy, crunchy crust, a crowd-pleaser. The brine tenderizes the meat, keeps it moist, and seasons it from the outside in.

Buttermilk Fried Chicken

- In a very large glass bowl, make a brine by whisking together the buttermilk, salt, and hot sauce until the salt dissolves. Add the chicken, making sure that it is completely submerged. Cover and refrigerate for 6–12 hours. Remove the bowl from the refrigerator about 1 hour before you plan to fry.

- Line a rimmed baking sheet with parchment paper. In a shallow dish, whisk together the flour, baking powder, black pepper, cayenne pepper, rosemary, thyme, and sage. One piece at a time, remove the chicken from the brine, shaking off the excess, and roll in the seasoned flour until completely coated. Place the coated chicken on the lined baking sheet.

- In a large, heavy, deep frying pan, preferably cast iron, pour the oil to a depth of 1 inch (2.5 cm) and insert the probe of a deep-frying thermometer into the oil. Heat over high heat until the thermometer reads 350°F (180°C). Preheat the oven to 350°F.

- When the oil is ready, using tongs, carefully add the drumsticks and thighs to the hot oil and fry until the undersides are golden brown, about 4 minutes. Using tongs, turn and cook until the second sides are golden brown, about 4 minutes longer. Transfer the pieces to a rimmed baking sheet, place in the oven, and bake for 10 minutes. Repeat to fry the breast pieces and wings in the same manner, then add to the baking sheet with the legs. Bake all the pieces until opaque in the center when pierced with a small knife, about 10 minutes longer.

- Drain the chicken briefly on paper towels and serve right away.

4 cups (32 fl oz/1 l) buttermilk

¼ cup (2½ oz/75 g) table salt

1 tbsp hot-pepper sauce

1 chicken, about 4 lb (2 kg), cut into 10 pieces

1 cup (5 oz/155 g) all-purpose flour

¾ tsp baking powder

½ tsp freshly ground black pepper

¼ tsp cayenne pepper

½ tsp dried rosemary, crushed

½ tsp dried thyme

½ tsp dried sage

Canola oil

MAKES 4 SERVINGS

With this recipe, you can have the satisfaction of fried chicken with only a fraction of the work. Chicken tenders cook in no time and, perched on a fresh green salad, make a light-but-satisfying meal.

Green Salad with Chicken Strips

● In a glass bowl, whisk together the vinegar, ½ teaspoon salt, and ¼ teaspoon black pepper. Whisk in the mustard. While whisking, add the the oil in a slow, steady stream until incorporated to make a dressing. Set aside.

● In a shallow dish, whisk together the flour, baking powder, 1 teaspoon salt, ½ teaspoon black pepper, the cayenne pepper, thyme, and sage. One at a time, coat the chicken tenders with the seasoned flour and shake off the excess. Transfer to a plate.

● Preheat the oven to 200°F (95°C). In a large, heavy, deep frying pan, preferably cast iron, pour the canola oil to a depth of 1 inch (2.5 cm) and insert the probe of a deep-frying thermometer into the oil. Heat over high heat until the thermometer reads 350°F (180°C).

● When the oil is ready, using tongs, add the chicken to the hot oil and fry until the undersides are golden brown, about 2½ minutes. Turn and cook until the second sides are golden brown, about 2½ minutes longer. Transfer to a rimmed baking sheet and keep warm in the oven.

● In a large bowl, combine the greens, tomatoes, and onion slices. Drizzle with the dressing and toss gently. Divide among serving plates, arrange the warm chicken on top, and serve right away.

1 tbsp red wine vinegar

Kosher salt and freshly ground black pepper

1 tsp Dijon mustard

3 tbsp extra-virgin olive oil

1 cup (5 oz/155 g) all-purpose flour

¾ tsp baking powder

¼ tsp cayenne pepper

½ tsp dried thyme

½ tsp dried sage

1½ lb (750 g) chicken tenders

Canola oil

4 cups (4 oz/120 g) mixed baby salad greens

2 cups (12 oz/375 g) grape tomatoes

½ red onion, thinly sliced

MAKES 4 SERVINGS

In this simple but elegant dish, sherry and cream elevate sautéed chicken breasts with an indulgent sauce. Choose a dry sherry, such as amontillado or fino, to strike the right flavor balance.

Chicken Breasts with Cream & Sherry

4 boneless, skinless
chicken breast halves
6 oz (185 g) each,
lightly pounded until
½ inch (12 mm) thick

Kosher salt and freshly
ground pepper

3 tbsp unsalted butter

1 tbsp canola oil

¼ cup (1½ oz/45 g)
all-purpose flour

1 shallot, minced

⅓ cup (3 fl oz/80 ml)
dry sherry

⅔ cup (5 fl oz/160 ml)
Chicken Stock
(page 138) or low-
sodium chicken broth

½ cup (4 fl oz/125 ml)
heavy cream

MAKES 4 SERVINGS

● Sprinkle both sides of the chicken breast halves with ½ teaspoon salt and ½ teaspoon pepper.

● Place a large frying pan over medium-high heat and add 1 tablespoon of the butter and the oil. Meanwhile, spread the flour in a shallow dish. One at a time, lightly coat the breasts in the flour, shaking off excess, and place the coated breasts in the pan.

● Cook until the undersides are golden brown, about 3 minutes. Turn and reduce the heat to medium. Sauté until the second sides are golden brown and the breasts feel firm when pressed in the center with a fingertip, about 3 minutes longer. Transfer to a warmed platter.

● Place the pan over medium heat and add 1 tablespoon of the butter. When the butter has melted, add the shallot and sauté until softened, about 2 minutes. Raise the heat to high, add the sherry, and bring just to a boil, scraping up the browned bits on the pan bottom. Add the stock and cream and cook until reduced by one-fourth, about 2 minutes.

● Return the breasts to the pan, turn once, and cook for 1 minute. Transfer the breasts to warmed individual plates. Off the heat, whisk in the remaining 1 tablespoon butter until melted. Taste and adjust the seasonings. Spoon the sauce over the chicken and serve right away.

Scoring the skin of duck breasts helps to release as much fat as possible during cooking, yielding crisp skin. Port and cherries make an intensely flavored sauce that complements the rich meat.

Duck Breasts with Cherries

4 cups (32 fl oz/1 l) Chicken Stock (page 138) or low-sodium chicken broth

1 cup (8 fl oz/250 ml) tawny or ruby Port

2 sprigs fresh rosemary

4 boneless duck breast halves, 12–14 oz (375–440 g) each

Kosher salt and freshly ground pepper

3 tbsp cold unsalted butter

1 shallot, minced

1 jar (12 oz/375 g) sour cherries in juice, juice drained and 2 tablespoons reserved

1 tsp cornstarch

MAKES 4–6 SERVINGS

● In a saucepan, boil the stock, Port, and rosemary sprigs until reduced to 1 cup (8 fl oz/250 ml), about 15 minutes. Strain through a sieve into a small bowl. Set aside.

● Score just the skin of the duck in a crosshatch pattern. Sprinkle both sides with 1 teaspoon salt and 2 teaspoons coarse pepper, then place skin side down in a large cold frying pan. Cook over medium-high heat until the skin is deeply browned, about 10 minutes. Transfer to a platter. Pour off the fat.

● Place the breasts skin side up in the pan, cover, and cook over medium heat until a breast half feels resilient when pressed, about 12 minutes for medium-rare. Transfer to a carving board, tent with aluminum foil, and let stand for 5 minutes.

● Pour off the fat in the pan. Place the pan over medium heat and add 1 tablespoon of the butter. Add the shallot and sauté until softened, about 2 minutes. Add the drained cherries and Port mixture, bring to a boil, and cook until slightly reduced, about 2 minutes.

● In a bowl, stir together the reserved cherry juice and cornstarch, then whisk the mixture into the pan. Cook just until thickened, about 10 seconds. Cut the remaining 2 tablespoons butter into cubes. Off the heat, whisk in the butter until melted.

● Slice the breasts across the grain and fan out the slices on warmed plates. Spoon the cherry sauce over the top and serve right away.

Grilling and broiling are versatile cooking methods. Both direct-heat grilling and broiling impart crisp surfaces and juicy centers by cooking chicken and other poultry directly over or under the heat source. Indirect-heat grilling, another popular method, cooks larger

Grilled & Broiled

pieces of poultry to a moist, even finish by employing reflected heat in a covered grill to mimic oven roasting. In this chapter, you'll find plenty of options for a delicious chicken dinner—from dishes inspired by international classics, to down-home favorites for your next cookout, to creative recipes for busy weeknights.

Cuts for Grilling & Broiling

A variety of poultry cuts work for grilling and broiling, from quick-cooking boneless chicken breasts to whole birds. Bone-in chicken pieces are the classic choice for barbecued chicken and similar recipes, as the bones contribute natural flavor and moisture. Butterflied chicken is also crisp and delicious on the grill.

Rubs & Flavored Butters

Cover the outside of poultry with a blend of spices or herbs to impart bold flavor directly onto the skin of the bird. Or, mix herbs and spices with butter and then apply under or on top of the skin to create flavor, moisture, and crispness. Either method creates vibrant flavor that contrasts nicely with the mild taste of poultry.

Marinades & Brines

Marinating and brining are popular methods for enhancing poultry, adding both flavor and moisture. For either method, choose a nonreactive bowl or large locking plastic bag and watch the clock—acids in marinades affect texture, and over-brining causes saltiness. Observe recipe times to ensure moist and flavorful results.

Tips & Tricks

Direct-Heat Cooking

Cooking foods directly over, or under, the heat source is referred to as direct-heat cooking. It is ideal for small, tender cuts of poultry that cook quickly. On a charcoal grill, place the food directly over the hot coals. On a gas grill, place the food directly over the heat element. When broiling, center the food directly under the heat source to ensure even cooking.

Indirect-Heat Grilling

Indirect-heat grilling is essential for larger or thicker cuts of poultry or whole birds that take a relatively long time to cook through. Be sure your grill has a cover, which, when closed, creates a convection motion that mimics an oven to cook foods from all sides. To impart a pronounced smoky flavor to your food, you can add wood chips to the hot part of the grill.

Gauging the Heat

Grilling is very forgiving. If you are using a charcoal grill, or if your gas grill does not have a built-in thermometer, hold your hand about 4 inches (10 cm) above the grill rack for as long as you comfortably can and count. High heat corresponds to 1 or 2 seconds; medium-high heat is reached at 2 or 3 seconds. When broiling, be sure to preheat for at least 15 minutes.

In this Italian-inspired method, a butterflied chicken is grilled under a heavy weight (traditionally a brick). This exposes all exterior areas of the bird to direct heat for deeply golden, crisp skin.

Tuscan-Style Chicken

- In a bowl, whisk together the lemon zest and juice, olive oil, garlic, oregano, ¾ teaspoon salt, and the red pepper flakes. Place the chicken in a shallow glass or ceramic dish, pour the marinade over the top, and turn to coat. Cover tightly and refrigerate for at least 30 minutes or up to 2 hours. Remove from the refrigerator 30 minutes before grilling.

- Prepare a grill for direct-heat cooking over medium heat (page 132). Have ready a heavy cast-iron frying pan or 2 bricks wrapped in aluminum foil.

- Lightly rub the grill grate with canola oil. Remove the chicken from the marinade and place skin side down on the grill. Discard the marinade. Place the pan on top of the chicken, cover the grill, and cook until the skin is golden brown, about 30 minutes. Turn over the chicken, replace the pan or bricks, and cover the grill. Cook for about 15 minutes longer.

- Remove the pan or bricks. Insert an instant-read thermometer into the thickest part of the thigh, not touching bone. It should read 170°F (77°C). If the chicken is not done, replace the pan on top, cover the grill, cook for another 5 minutes, and then test again. Transfer the chicken to a carving board let rest for 5 minutes.

- Using a chef's knife and firm pressure, cut the chicken in half lengthwise through the breastbone. Then, cut each portion in half where the breast area meets the thigh. Serve right away with lemon wedges.

2 tsp grated lemon zest

⅓ cup (3 fl oz/80 ml) fresh lemon juice

2 tbsp extra-virgin olive oil

3 cloves garlic, chopped

1 tsp dried oregano

Kosher salt

¾ tsp red pepper flakes

1 large chicken, about 4 lb (2 kg), butterflied (page 121)

Canola oil

Lemon wedges

MAKES 4 SERVINGS

This spicy, refreshing dish takes inspiration from the cuisine of the West Indian island of Saint Lucia. Flavorful, with just a touch of sweetness, the chicken is beautifully complemented by a fruit salsa.

Spiced Chicken, Island-Style

- In a bowl, stir together the brown sugar and hot water until the sugar dissolves. Add the parsley, cilantro, thyme, cumin, turmeric, curry powder, olive oil, garlic, and onion and mix well.

- Place the chicken pieces in a shallow glass or ceramic dish. Spoon the marinade over the chicken, turning to coat evenly. Cover and refrigerate for 24 hours, turning several times. Remove the chicken from the refrigerator 30 minutes before grilling.

- Prepare a grill for direct-heat cooking over high heat (page 132).

- Lightly rub the grill grate with canola oil. Place the drumsticks and thighs on the hot part of the grill, cover, and cook, turning once, until browned, about 7 minutes on each side. Move the pieces to the cool part of the grill and place the breasts and wings on the hot part. Cover and cook until browned, about 8 minutes. Turn over all the pieces and continue to cook until the skin is crisp and the juices run clear when a thigh is pierced with a knife, about 8 minutes longer.

- Transfer to a warmed platter and serve right away accompanied by the salsa.

3 tbsp firmly packed dark brown sugar

⅓ cup (3 fl oz/80 ml) hot water

2 tbsp chopped fresh flat-leaf parsley

1 tbsp chopped fresh cilantro

½ tsp chopped fresh thyme

½ tsp *each* ground cumin, turmeric, and curry powder

4 tsp olive oil

1 large clove garlic, minced

1 yellow onion, halved and sliced

2 chickens, about 3½ lb (1.75 kg) each, cut into 8 pieces

Canola oil

Mango Salsa, page 139

MAKES 6 SERVINGS

This spicy-sweet sauce offers the best flavors of traditional southern barbecue with just a touch of Latin-style heat. Ancho chiles have a sweet, earthy flavor that improves with smoky notes from the grill.

Chile-Spiked Chicken

1 ancho chile, seeded, cut into pieces, and soaked in 1 cup (8 fl oz/ 250 ml) boiling water for 20 minutes

1 tbsp olive oil

2 chickens, about 3½ lb (1.75 kg) each, cut into 8 pieces

2 tbsp unsalted butter

1 yellow onion, finely chopped

1½ cups (12 fl oz/ 375 ml) ketchup

⅓ cup (3 fl oz/80 ml) Worcestershire sauce

¼ cup (2 fl oz/60 ml) steak sauce

2 tbsp cider vinegar

⅓ cup (2½ oz/75 g) firmly packed golden brown sugar

Canola oil

MAKES 6 SERVINGS

● Drain the chile and add to a food processor with ¼ cup (2 fl oz/60 ml) of the soaking liquid and the olive oil. Process until a thick, smooth paste forms. Rub the chicken with the paste and place in a shallow glass or ceramic dish. Cover and refrigerate for 2–24 hours. Remove from the refrigerator 30 minutes before grilling.

● In a saucepan over medium heat, melt the butter. Add the onion and sauté until softened, about 5 minutes. Stir in the ketchup, ¼ cup (4 fl oz/125 ml) water, the Worcestershire sauce, steak sauce, vinegar, and brown sugar. Bring to a boil, reduce the heat to low, cover partially, and simmer until thickened slightly, about 20 minutes. Set aside.

● Prepare a grill for direct-heat cooking over high heat (page 132).

● Lightly rub the grill rack with canola oil. Place the drumsticks and thighs on the hot part of the grill, cover, and cook, turning once, until browned, about 7 minutes per side. Move to the cool part of the grill and place the breasts and wings on the hot part. Cover and cook until browned, about 8 minutes. Turn over all the pieces and cook until the juices run clear when a thigh is pierced, about 8 minutes longer.

● Brush the chicken with ¼ cup (2 fl oz/60 ml) of the sauce, then turn over and brush with another ¼ cup sauce. Cook until crisp, about 2 minutes on each side.

● Transfer to a warmed platter and serve right away, passing the remaining sauce at the table.

Traditional tandoori chicken involves a special, charcoal-fueled clay oven. A smoky outdoor grill yields similar results, concentrating the yogurt-and-spice marinade to create a savory golden coating.

Indian-Style Chicken Thighs

8 bone-in, skinless chicken thighs, about 3 lb (1.5 kg) total weight

2 tbsp fresh lemon juice

Kosher salt

2 cloves garlic

1 small yellow onion, coarsely chopped

1 cup (8 oz/250 g) plain yogurt

1 tbsp high-quality curry powder

1 tsp sweet Hungarian paprika

¼ tsp ground cinnamon

Canola oil

MAKES 4 SERVINGS

● In a glass bowl, toss together the chicken thighs and lemon juice. Sprinkle with ¾ teaspoon salt and mix well. Cover and refrigerate for 1 hour.

● With a food processor running, drop the garlic through the feed tube to chop it. Add the onion and pulse until puréed. Add the yogurt, curry powder, paprika, and cinnamon and pulse to combine. Pour over the chicken and stir well. Cover and refrigerate for 4–12 hours. Remove from the refrigerator 30 minutes before cooking.

● Prepare a grill for indirect-heat cooking over medium-high heat (page 133).

● Lightly rub the grill grate with canola oil. Remove the thighs from the marinade and place, skinned side up, on the cool side of the grill. Discard the marinade. Cover and cook, without turning, until an instant-read thermometer inserted in the thickest part of a thigh, not touching bone, reads 170°F (77°C), 25–35 minutes.

● Transfer to a warmed platter and let rest for 5 minutes. Serve right away.

Here, chicken is soaked in a Mexican-style marinade before grilling. Tucked into soft tortillas with sharp cheese, crisp lettuce, and spicy salsa, these are a great alternative to everyday barbecue fare.

Chicken Tacos

- In a small bowl, mix together the cumin, oregano, and ½ teaspoon salt. Sprinkle the mixture evenly over both sides of the chicken, then drizzle with the olive oil and lime juice. Set aside.

- Prepare a grill for direct-heat cooking over medium-high heat (page 132).

- Lightly rub the grill grate with canola oil. Add the chicken to the grill and cook until opaque throughout, 3–4 minutes per side. During the last minute of grilling, add the tortillas to the grill, directly over the heat, and cook, turning once, until heated through and flexible. Transfer the chicken to a cutting board and the tortillas to a plate. Let the chicken rest for 5 minutes.

- Cut the chicken breast into bite-sized pieces. To assemble the tacos, add a few pieces of chicken to each tortilla, top with cheese, lettuce, and salsa, dividing evenly, and serve right away.

¼ tsp ground cumin

¼ tsp dried oregano

Kosher salt

¾ lb (375 g) boneless, skinless chicken breast halves

1 tbsp olive oil

Juice of 1 lime

Canola oil

12 corn tortillas

1 cup (4 oz/125 g) shredded sharp Cheddar cheese

½ head romaine lettuce, shredded

1 cup (8 fl oz/250 ml) Fresh Tomato Salsa (page 139)

MAKES 4 SERVINGS

This fresh Asian-inspired noodle salad, hearty with grilled chicken and fresh vegetables, is perfect for a light supper on a hot summer evening. Adjust the amount of chile sauce according to your taste.

Chicken with Sesame Noodles

¼ cup (2 fl oz/60 ml) *each* rice vinegar, soy sauce, and canola oil

3 tbsp orange juice

2 tbsp brown sugar

1½ tbsp Asian sesame oil

1 tbsp minced garlic

1–2 tsp chile-garlic sauce, such as Sriracha

¾ lb (375 g) boneless, skinless chicken breast halves

Kosher salt and freshly ground pepper

1 cup (5 oz/155 g) shelled edamame

1 lb (500 g) fresh Asian egg noodles

2 carrots, grated

¼ cup (¾ oz/20 g) sliced green onions

2 tbsp sesame seeds

MAKES 6 SERVINGS

● In a bowl, mix the vinegar, soy sauce, ¼ cup (2 fl oz/60 ml) canola oil, the orange juice, brown sugar, sesame oil, garlic, and chile-garlic sauce to make a dressing. Set aside 2 tablespoons for the chicken and reserve the rest. Season the chicken lightly with salt and pepper and brush it with the 2 tablespoons dressing.

● Prepare a grill for direct-heat cooking over medium-high heat (page 132).

● Lightly rub the grill grate with canola oil. Add the chicken to the grill and cook until opaque throughout, 3–4 minutes per side. Transfer the chicken to a cutting board and, when cool enough to handle, cut it into strips about 2 inches (5 cm) long and ½ inch (12 mm) wide.

● Bring a large pot of water to a boil. Add the edamame and cook until just tender, 2–3 minutes. Remove the edamame with a slotted spoon, drain well, and bring the water back to a boil. Add the noodles and cook until tender, 3–4 minutes. Drain well.

● In a large bowl, toss together the noodles, chicken strips, remaining dressing, edamame, carrots, green onions, and sesame seeds. Serve right away.

Broiling is a fast and delicious way to cook chicken, as it quickly crisps the skin. Here, a mixture of pungent mustard, sweet tarragon, and heady garlic creates a delicious coating on the pieces.

Chicken with Mustard-Herb Topping

● Preheat the broiler for 10–15 minutes. Have ready a 2-piece broiler pan and coat the rack well with canola oil.

● Pat the chicken breasts dry with paper towels and sprinkle both sides with ½ teaspoon salt. In a small bowl, stir together the mustard, garlic, tarragon, and chives until well blended.

● Place the breasts, skin side down, on the oiled broiler rack. Broil until the exposed flesh of the breasts is golden brown, about 10 minutes.

● Remove the broiler pan and place it on the stove top. Using tongs, turn the chicken breasts skin side up. Spread the mustard mixture evenly over the chicken skin. Return the breasts to the broiler and broil until the coating is deep golden brown and an instant-read thermometer inserted into the thickest part of a breast, not touching bone, reads 170°F (77°C), 5–10 minutes longer.

● Transfer to a warmed platter and let stand for 5 minutes. Serve right away.

Canola oil

6 bone-in, skin-on chicken breast halves, about ½ lb (250 g) each

Kosher salt

5 tbsp Dijon mustard

2 cloves garlic, minced

4 tsp chopped fresh tarragon

1 tbsp snipped fresh chives

MAKES 6 SERVINGS

Brined olives bring bold flavor to mild chicken. Assertive tapenade, the provençal olive paste, stars in this recipe. On busy nights, use ¾ cup (6 fl oz/180 ml) purchased tapenade instead of homemade.

Tapenade-Stuffed Chicken Breasts

● Preheat the broiler for 10–15 minutes. Have ready a 2-piece broiler pan and coat the rack well with canola oil.

● Pat the chicken breasts dry with paper towels. Starting at the widest side of each breast, slip your fingers under the skin to loosen it, keeping it attached on the opposite side. Spread an equal amount of the tapenade under the skin of each chicken breast.

● Place the breasts, skin side down, on the oiled broiler rack. Broil until the exposed flesh of the breasts is golden brown, about 10 minutes.

● Remove the broiler pan and place it on the stove top. Using tongs, turn the chicken breasts skin side up. Return the breasts to the broiler and broil until the skin is deep golden brown and an instant-read thermometer inserted into the thickest part of a breast, not touching bone, reads 170°F (77°C), 5–10 minutes longer.

● Transfer to a warmed platter and let stand for 5 minutes. Serve right away.

Canola oil

4 bone-in, skin-on chicken breast halves, about ½ lb (250 g) each

Tapenade, page 138

MAKES 4 SERVINGS

Pesto slipped under the skin of chicken breasts packs big flavor in this quick recipe. If you are short on time, use ¾ cup (6 fl oz/180 ml) of your favorite purchased pesto instead of the one here.

Pesto-Stuffed Chicken Breasts

Canola oil

4 bone-in, skin-on chicken breast halves, about ½ lb (250 g) each

Pesto, page 139

MAKES 4 SERVINGS

- Preheat the broiler for 10–15 minutes. Have ready a 2-piece broiler pan and coat the rack well with canola oil.

- Pat the chicken breasts dry with paper towels. Starting at the widest side of each breast, slip your fingers under the skin to loosen it, keeping it attached on the opposite side. Spread an equal amount of the pesto under the skin of each breast.

- Place the breasts, skin side down, on the oiled broiler rack. Broil until the exposed flesh of the breasts is golden brown, about 10 minutes.

- Remove the broiler pan and place it on the stove top. Using tongs, turn the chicken breasts skin side up. Return the breasts to the broiler and broil until the skin is deep golden brown and an instant-read thermometer inserted into the thickest part of a breast, not touching bone, reads 170°F (77°C), 5–10 minutes longer.

- Transfer to a warmed platter and let stand for 5 minutes. Serve right away.

An aromatic sage butter applied under the skin of a turkey breast contributes to the bird's succulence. Cooking over an outdoor fire adds an irresistible smoky flavor. Serve with grilled vegetables.

Turkey Breast with Sage Butter

1 bone-in, skin-on turkey breast half, about 3 lb (1.5 kg)

3 tbsp unsalted butter, at room temperature

1 tbsp finely chopped fresh sage

Kosher salt and freshly ground pepper

Canola oil

MAKES 6 SERVINGS

● About 30 minutes before grilling, remove the turkey from the refrigerator. Prepare a grill for indirect-heat cooking over medium-high heat (page 133).

● In a small bowl, mash together the butter and sage. Pat the turkey breast dry with paper towels. Using your hands, rub the sage butter evenly all over the turkey skin. Sprinkle 3/4 teaspoon salt and 1/2 teaspoon pepper evenly over both sides of the turkey breast.

● Lightly rub the grill grate with canola oil. Place the turkey, skin side up, on the cool part of the grill. Cover and cook until an instant-read thermometer inserted in the thickest part of the breast, not touching bone, reads 170°F (77°C), about 1 hour.

● Transfer the breast, skin side up, to a carving board and let rest for 10 minutes. Using a thin, flexible carving knife, cut the breast meat away from the rib cage in a single piece. Cut the breast across the grain into slices 1/2 inch (12 mm) thick. As the slices are cut, arrange them on a warmed platter.

● If desired, pour any accumulated juices on the carving board over the turkey slices. Serve right away.

Chicken takes on a mahogany finish when brushed with this Asian-style glaze. The saltiness of the soy sauce complements the smoky flavor from the fire. Both mirin and dry sake add depth to the glaze.

Soy-Glazed Chicken Breasts

● Prepare a grill for direct-heat cooking over medium-high heat (page 132).

● In a small saucepan over high heat, stir together the soy sauce, mirin, sake, ginger, garlic, and brown sugar and bring to a boil. Boil for 1 minute, then remove from the heat, pour into a shallow bowl, and let cool completely.

● About 15 minutes before the fire is ready, set aside about ¼ cup (2 fl oz/160 ml) of the soy mixture to use for basting. Then, place the chicken breasts in the remaining cooled soy mixture.

● Lightly rub the grill grate with canola oil. Remove the chicken from the marinade and place on the grill rack. Discard the marinade. Cook, turning once and brushing with the reserved soy mixture, until the chicken is opaque throughout and the juices run clear when pierced with a knife tip, about 4 minutes per side.

● Transfer the chicken to a warmed platter and serve right away sprinkled with the green onions and sesame seeds.

½ cup (4 fl oz/125 ml) soy sauce

¼ cup (2 fl oz/60 ml) mirin

¼ cup (2 fl oz/60 ml) dry sake or dry sherry

1 tbsp peeled and chopped fresh ginger

2 cloves garlic, minced

1 tsp brown sugar

4 skinless, boneless chicken breast halves, about 6 oz (185 g) each, pounded until ½ inch (12 mm) thick

Canola oil

1–2 green onions, thinly sliced on the diagonal

1 tsp sesame seeds, toasted

MAKES 4 SERVINGS

Tart lime juice balances the spiciness of the chili powder in this bold marinade. The strong flavors also mean a shorter marinating time, bringing added convenience for weeknight meals.

Chili-Lime Chicken

4 bone-in, skin-on chicken breast halves, about ½ lb (250 g) each

2 tbsp extra-virgin olive oil

4 tsp chili powder

Grated zest of 1 lime

2 tbsp fresh lime juice

1 clove garlic, minced

Kosher salt

Canola oil

MAKES 4 SERVINGS

● Pat dry the chicken breasts with paper towels. In a large, shallow glass or ceramic dish, stir together the olive oil, chili powder, lime zest and juice, garlic, and ¾ teaspoon salt. Add the chicken breasts, turn to coat evenly, cover, and refrigerate for 1–8 hours.

● Preheat the broiler for 10–15 minutes. Have ready a 2-piece broiler pan and coat the rack well with canola oil.

● Place the breasts, skin side down, on the oiled broiler rack. Broil until the exposed flesh of the breasts is golden brown, about 10 minutes.

● Remove the broiler pan and place it on the stove top. Using tongs, turn the chicken breasts skin side up. Return the breasts to the broiler and broil until the skin is deep golden brown and an instant-read thermometer inserted into the thickest part of a breast, not touching bone, reads 170°F (77°C), 5–10 minutes longer.

● Transfer to a warmed platter and let stand for 5 minutes. Serve right away.

The dipping sauce that accompanies these skewers is rich, creamy, and packed with complex flavors. The tender but mild chicken spends time in a marinade that carries the same bold seasonings.

Chicken Skewers with Peanut Sauce

- Soak 24 short wooden skewers in water to cover for 30 minutes. In a blender, blend the vinegar, lime juice, garlic, ginger, chile, and mint until a smooth purée forms. With the blender running, slowly add the peanut and sesame oils through the feed hole in the lid until a thick mixture forms.

- Place the chicken in a shallow glass dish. Add 3 tablespoons of the ginger-chile mixture and toss to coat. Cover and refrigerate, stirring occasionally, for 2 hours. Meanwhile, add the peanut butter and soy sauce to the blender with the remaining mixture and blend until well mixed. Taste and adjust the seasonings. Set aside.

- About 20 minutes before broiling, remove the chicken from the refrigerator. Preheat the broiler for 10–15 minutes. Have ready a 2-piece broiler pan and coat the rack well with canola oil.

- Thread 1 piece of chicken onto each skewer, poking it lengthwise through the center of each piece so the skewers can lie flat. Arrange the skewers on the oiled broiler rack without touching. Broil, turning once, until the chicken is just firm to the touch and opaque throughout, about 4 minutes total.

- Sprinkle both sides of the chicken with ⅛ teaspoon salt. Garnish with the green onion and serve right away with the dipping sauce.

2 tbsp rice vinegar

1 tbsp fresh lime juice

3 large cloves garlic

2 tsp minced
fresh ginger

½ jalapeño chile,
seeded and minced

3 tbsp coarsely
chopped fresh mint

3 tbsp *each* peanut oil
and Asian sesame oil

1½ lb (560 g) boneless,
skinless chicken breast
halves, lightly pounded
and cut into 1-inch
(2.5-cm) squares

⅓ cup (3½ oz/105 g)
smooth peanut butter

1 tbsp soy sauce

Canola oil

Kosher salt

1 green onion,
thinly sliced

MAKES 4 SERVINGS

Traditional Jamaican jerk treatments are dry rubs. In this recipe, bold jerk spices are made into a wet marinade, which helps to preserve moisture when cooking over the direct heat of an outdoor grill.

Jerk Chicken Skewers

- Soak 32 short wooden skewers in water to cover for 30 minutes.

- In a food processor, process the green onions, chile, garlic, canola oil, lime juice, soy sauce, thyme, and allspice until blended.

- Place the chicken strips in a shallow glass dish. Drizzle the green onion-chile mixture over the chicken and turn to coat. Cover and let marinate at room temperature for 30 minutes.

- Prepare a grill for direct-heat cooking grilling over high heat (page 132). Wearing rubber gloves to prevent your hands from coming in contact with the spicy marinade, if desired, weave the chicken strips onto the skewers, accordion style.

- Lightly rub the grill grate with canola oil. Place the chicken on the grill and cook, turning once, until opaque throughout, about 6 minutes total. Transfer to a warmed platter and serve right away.

6 green onions, minced

½ Scotch bonnet chile, seeded, deribbed, and minced

4 cloves garlic, minced

¼ cup (2 fl oz/60 ml) canola oil plus oil for the grill

¼ cup (2 fl oz/60 ml) fresh lime juice

2 tbsp soy sauce

2 tsp dried thyme

1 tsp ground allspice

2 lb (1 kg) boneless, skinless chicken breast halves, lightly pounded and cut into strips ½ inch (12 mm) wide and 2 inches (5 cm) long

MAKES 4–6 SERVINGS

Chicken cubes and summer vegetables are marinated in the characteristic seasonings of the Greek Isles then are threaded onto skewers and grilled. Round out the meal with rice pilaf.

Lemon-Oregano Chicken Kebabs

1 Asian eggplant

1 red bell pepper

1 yellow onion

½ cup (4 fl oz/125 ml) fresh lemon juice

¼ cup (2 fl oz/60 ml) dry white wine

2 tbsp olive oil

2 cloves garlic, minced

2 tbsp chopped fresh oregano

Grated zest of ½ lemon

Kosher salt and freshly ground pepper

1½ lb (750 g) boneless, skinless, chicken breast halves, cut into 1½-inch (4-cm) cubes

Canola oil

Lemon wedges

MAKES 4 SERVINGS

- Cut the eggplant crosswise into slices. Seed the red pepper and cut it into 1-inch (2.5-cm) squares. Cut the onion in half, separate it into layers, then cut into 1½-inch (4-cm) squares.

- In a shallow glass dish, combine the lemon juice, wine, olive oil, garlic, oregano, lemon zest, ½ teaspoon salt, and ¼ teaspoon pepper. Add the chicken, eggplant, pepper, and onion and toss to coat. Cover and refrigerate, stirring occasionally, for about 1 hour.

- Soak 8 long wooden skewers in water to cover for 30 minutes. About 20 minutes before grilling, remove the chicken from the refrigerator. Prepare a grill for indirect-heat cooking over medium-high heat (page 133). Thread the chicken, eggplant, bell pepper, and onion pieces onto the skewers, alternating the vegetable pieces and dividing them equally.

- Lightly rub the grill grate with canola oil. Place the skewers on the hot part of the grill and cook, turning once or twice, until the chicken is browned, about 5 minutes total. Move the skewers to the cool part of the grill, cover, and cook, turning occasionally, until the chicken is opaque throughout and the vegetables are tender, 10–15 minutes.

- Transfer the skewers to a warmed platter or individual plates and serve right away with the lemon wedges.

Rich duck stands up well to this amalgam of Southwestern flavors: smoky chipotle, dusky sage, piquant jalapeño, and tart citrus. Weighting the breasts with a pan during grilling helps crisp the skin.

Chipotle-Orange Duck Breasts

4 boneless duck breast halves, 12–14 oz (375–440 g) each

Grated zest of 2 large oranges

2 tbsp fresh orange juice

2 tbsp finely chopped fresh sage

2 tbsp extra-virgin olive oil

1 tsp ground chipotle chile

Kosher salt

Canola oil

MAKES 4 SERVINGS

● Using a sharp, thin-bladed knife, score the skin of the duck in a crosshatch pattern, taking care not to cut into the meat.

● In a small bowl, stir together the orange zest and juice, sage, olive oil, chipotle powder, and 1 teaspoon salt. Spread the mixture evenly over both sides of each breast, cover, and let stand at room temperature for 1 hour.

● Prepare a grill for indirect-heat cooking over medium-high heat (page 133). Have ready a heavy flameproof frying pan, preferably cast iron.

● When the fire is hot, lightly rub the grill grate with canola oil and lightly oil the bottom of the frying pan. Place the duck breasts, flesh side down, on the hot part of the grill and cook until the flesh is seared with grill marks, about 2 minutes. Turn the breasts and cook until the skin is browned slightly, about 2 minutes. Transfer the breasts, skin side down, to the cool area of the grill, and place the frying pan on top. Cover and cook until an instant-read thermometer inserted in the thickest part of the breast reads 135°–140°F (57°–60°C), about 10 minutes longer. Transfer the duck to a carving board and let rest for 5 minutes.

● Slice the breasts on the diagonal across the grain and fan out on warmed plates. Serve right away.

Evocative of barbecue in the southern U.S., this recipe pairs a sweet-hot sauce with grilled chicken. The sauce can be made in advance and stored tightly covered in the refrigerator for up to 2 weeks.

Southern-Style Grilled Chicken

- Prepare a grill for indirect-heat cooking over medium-high heat (page 133).

- Meanwhile, in a small saucepan over medium-high heat, combine the onion, half of the garlic, ketchup, vinegar, brown sugar, mustard, hot-pepper sauce, and Worcestershire sauce. Bring to a boil, stirring often. Reduce the heat to low and simmer, uncovered, until the sauce is thick and the flavors are blended, about 15 minutes. Set aside.

- In a small bowl, stir together the remaining garlic, paprika, 1 teaspoon salt, the cayenne pepper, and ½ teaspoon black pepper. Rub the mixture on the chicken, coating evenly, and set aside at room temperature until ready to grill.

- Lightly rub the grill grate with canola oil. Place the chicken on the hot part of the grill. Cook, turning once, until seared on both sides with grill marks, about 4 minutes total. Transfer the chicken pieces to a platter and spoon the sauce evenly over them.

- Return the chicken to the grill, positioning the pieces over the area with no heat. Cover and cook, turning once, until the chicken is opaque throughout and the juices run clear when pierced with a knife tip, about 20 minutes for the breasts and wings and 25 minutes for the thighs and drumsticks.

- Transfer the chicken pieces to a clean warmed platter and serve right away.

½ yellow onion, chopped

2 cloves garlic, minced

1 cup (8 fl oz/250 ml) ketchup

⅓ cup (3 fl oz/80 ml) red wine vinegar

¼ cup (2 oz/60 g) firmly packed light brown sugar

1 tbsp yellow mustard

2 tsp hot-pepper sauce

1 tsp Worcestershire sauce

1½ tsp sweet paprika

Kosher salt and freshly ground black pepper

1 tsp cayenne pepper

1 chicken, about 3½ lb (1.75 kg), cut into 8 pieces

Canola oil

MAKES 3–4 SERVINGS

Fajitas are a favorite in Tex-Mex cuisine. Steak is the traditional meat, but lightly marinated chicken breasts are a great stand-in for a light meal. Adjust the amount of chile to your taste.

Chicken Fajitas

2 cloves garlic, minced

1 jalapeño chile, seeded and minced

¼ cup (2 fl oz/60 ml) fresh lime juice

3 tbsp olive oil

1 tbsp chili powder

1 tbsp ground cumin

1 lb (500 g) boneless, skinless chicken breast halves

Canola oil

1 *each* large red and yellow bell pepper, quartered lengthwise and seeded

6 green onions

12 flour tortillas

Kosher salt and freshly ground pepper

Guacamole (page 139)

MAKES 4 SERVINGS

● In a shallow nonreactive dish, combine the garlic, chile, lime juice, olive oil, chili powder, and cumin. Add the chicken and turn to coat well. Let stand for 15 minutes.

● Prepare a grill for direct-heat cooking over medium-high heat (page 132).

● Lightly rub the grill grate with canola oil. Add the peppers and onions to the marinade with the chicken and stir to coat well.

● Place the chicken on the center of the grill. Place the vegetables around the perimeter. Cook, turning once or twice, until the chicken is opaque throughout and the vegetables are tender and lightly charred, 6–8 minutes total.

● Transfer the chicken and vegetables to a carving board and let rest for 5 minutes. Meanwhile, wrap the tortillas in aluminum foil and place on the grill until heated through, about 2 minutes.

● Cut the chicken and vegetables into thin strips and arrange on a warmed platter. Accompany with the tortillas and Guacamole. Guests can assemble their own fajitas by wrapping the ingredients in the tortillas.

If desired, use apple wood to impart a sweet smoky scent and complement the cider in the brine for this unique recipe. The smoke tends to darken the chicken skin more than when roasted.

Grill-Roasted Whole Chicken

In a nonreactive saucepan over high heat, combine the cider, salt, brown sugar, rosemary, peppercorns, and bay leaf. Bring to a boil, stirring to dissolve the salt and sugar. Remove from the heat, transfer to a large Dutch oven, and stir in the ice water until melted. Carefully lower the chicken into the brine, place a plate on top of the chicken to submerge it in the brine, and cover. Refrigerate for 8–12 hours.

Remove the chicken from the brine. Rinse and drain the chicken well, pat very dry, and let stand at room temperature for 30 minutes.

Place the wood chips in a bowl and add enough water to cover completely. If you are using a gas grill, have an additional handful of dry, unsoaked chips ready to use as a starter for the soaked chips. Prepare a grill for indirect-heat cooking over medium-high heat (page 133).

Add a handful of soaked, drained chips to the grill (page 133). Lightly rub the grill grate with oil. Place the chicken, breast side up, on the grill grate over the drip pan. Cover and cook, without turning, for 45 minutes. Uncover, add another handful of soaked chips, and re-cover the grill. Continue to cook until an instant-read thermometer inserted where the thigh meets the drumstick, not touching bone, reads 170°F (77°C), 45–60 minutes longer.

Transfer the chicken, breast side up, to a carving board and let rest for 10 minutes. Carve the bird, divide among warmed plates, and serve right away.

1½ cups (12 fl oz/375 ml) hard apple cider

½ cup (4 oz/125 g) table salt

⅓ cup (3½ oz/105 g) firmly packed light brown sugar

2 tbsp dried rosemary

1 tsp peppercorns

1 bay leaf

6½ cups (52 fl oz/1.6 l) ice water

1 large chicken, about 6 lb (3 kg)

2–3 handfuls apple or hickory wood chips

Canola oil

MAKES 6 SERVINGS

For your next cookout, try a quick and delicious dry rub to flavor a turkey breast. The zesty blend of spices delivers bold flavor to the meat, which is deepened by the smoke from the grill.

BBQ-Spiced Turkey Breast

- About 30 minutes before grilling, remove the turkey from the refrigerator. Prepare a grill for indirect-heat cooking over medium-high heat (page 133).

- In a small bowl, stir together the paprika, cumin, oregano, onion powder, garlic powder, chipotle, ½ teaspoon salt, and ¼ teaspoon black pepper. Add the butter and mash together until blended. Spread the spiced butter evenly over the turkey skin. Sprinkle both sides of the turkey breast with ½ teaspoon salt.

- Lightly rub the grill grate with canola oil. Place the turkey, skin side up, on the cool part of the grill. Cover and cook until an instant-read thermometer inserted in the thickest part of the breast, not touching bone, reads 170°F (77°C), about 1 hour.

- Transfer the breast, skin side up, to a carving board and let rest for 10 minutes. Using a thin, flexible carving knife, cut the breast meat away from the rib cage in a single piece. Cut the breast across the grain into slices ½ inch (12 mm) thick. As the slices are cut, arrange them on a warmed platter.

- If desired, pour any accumulated juices on the carving board over the turkey. Serve right away.

1 bone-in, skin-on turkey breast half, about 3 lb (1.5 kg)

2 tsp smoked Spanish paprika

1 tsp ground cumin

1 tsp dried oregano

¼ tsp onion powder

¼ tsp garlic powder

¼ tsp ground chipotle chile or cayenne pepper

Kosher salt and freshly ground black pepper

3 tbsp unsalted butter, at room temperature

Canola oil

MAKES 6 SERVINGS

Maple syrup is a great flavoring on the grill, lending distinctive sweet overtones to this peppery-smoky combination. Grade B maple syrup, which has a deep maple flavor, is preferred for this recipe.

Maple-Pepper Turkey Breast

1 bone-in, skin-on
turkey breast half,
about 3 lb (1.5 kg)

3 tbsp unsalted butter,
at room temperature

Kosher salt

¼ cup (3 oz/90 g)
maple syrup

½ tsp coarsely cracked
peppercorns

Canola oil

MAKES 6 SERVINGS

● About 30 minutes before grilling, remove the turkey from the refrigerator. Prepare a grill for indirect-heat cooking over medium-high heat (page 133).

● Spread the butter evenly over the skin of the turkey breast. Sprinkle both sides of the breast with ¾ teaspoon salt. In a small bowl, stir together the maple syrup and peppercorns.

● Lightly rub the grill grate with canola oil. Place the turkey, skin side up, on the cool part of the grill. Cover and cook until an instant-read thermometer inserted in the thickest part of the breast, not touching bone, reads 170°F (77°C), about 1 hour. During the last 10 minutes of grilling, brush the skin with the maple syrup mixture.

● Transfer the breast, skin side up, to a carving board and let rest for 10 minutes. Using a thin, flexible carving knife, cut the breast meat away from the rib cage in a single piece. Cut the breast across the grain into slices ½ inch (12 mm) thick. As the slices are cut, arrange them on a warmed platter.

● If desired, pour any accumulated juices on the carving board over the turkey. Serve right away.

Roasting and baking involve cooking foods in a pan in the dry, radiant heat of an enclosed oven. Time-pressed cooks like roasting because many foods can be cooked in under an hour. Also, once the initial prep is done, you can concentrate on preparing the rest

Roasted & Baked

of the meal while the poultry cooks largely unattended. Both techniques offer concentrated flavors and golden brown exteriors. Roasting and baking can be used for any occasion. Whether you are preparing a simple family weeknight supper or a lavish Saturday dinner for company, roasting sets the stage for a memorable meal.

Cuts for Roasting & Baking

Whole birds are well suited for roasting and can be prepared in a variety of ways: from simple seasonings to brines, marinades, glazes, and other flavorings. Poultry parts, too, are good candidates for roasting and baking. A butterflied bird roasts to a crisp finish in the high heat of the oven in less time than a whole bird.

Roasting vs. Baking

The differences between roasting and baking are not clear cut. Some believe roasting involves the use of fat while baking does not. Others claim baking is done in a covered pan while roasting is done in an uncovered pan. In either case, the techniques both utilize the dry heat of the oven to achieve moist interiors and well browned exteriors.

Preparing to Cook

Allow whole birds to stand at room temperature for about 30 minutes before roasting. This brings up the temperature slightly and promotes even roasting. Choose a pan that is just large enough to hold the poultry. If the food is too crowded, it will steam and not brown. A too large pan will cause the drippings to burn.

Tips & Tricks

Roasting Racks

An adjustable, V-shaped rack is an essential tool. The sides can be lifted to make a V formation for holding a whole bird, especially one that is turned during roasting, or they can be laid flat for roasting meats. The rack also folds up for easy storage. A flat-bottom rack works in a pinch. The key is to elevate the food off the bottom of the pan, promoting even roasting.

Under-the-Skin Seasoning

Slip your fingers under the skin of chicken or turkey breasts to tuck in flavored butters (page 123). The mixture infuses the poultry with flavor, while the skin protects the seasonings from drying and scorching. Keep one side of the skin attached when loosening, so it will stay in place as the chicken cooks. Be sure to wash your hands well after handling poultry.

Glazes, Sauces & Gravies

Glazing poultry during the final five to ten minutes of cooking adds a bright taste. Flavorful drippings can create elegant pan sauces and home-style gravies (page 126). The key to a good pan sauce is to degrease the clear fat from the juices so you are left with the dark, concentrated drippings. Dissolved in a flavorful liquid, they lend unmatched flavor to the sauce.

Perfect roast chicken with crisp skin and juicy flesh does not have to be a huge production. Savvy cooks know that prepping the bird requires little time, so you can rest easy with dinner in the oven.

Classic Roast Chicken

● Preheat the oven to 450°F (230°C). Brush a V-shaped roasting rack with oil and place in a flameproof roasting pan. Pat dry the chicken, then rub evenly with the room-temperature butter. Sprinkle evenly with ¾ teaspoon salt and ½ teaspoon pepper. Slip the rosemary into the cavity. Tuck each wing behind the shoulders of the bird and place on its back on the oiled rack.

● Roast the bird for 15 minutes. Turn the chicken onto one of its sides, reduce the oven temperature to 375°F (190°C) and roast until an instant-read thermometer inserted into the thickest part of the thigh, not touching bone, reads 170°F (77°C), about 60 minutes longer, turning the bird to its other side halfway through. Transfer the chicken, breast side up, to a carving board and let rest for 10–20 minutes.

● Pour the drippings from the roasting pan into a gravy separator or 2-cup (16–fl oz/ 500-ml) heatproof glass measuring cup. Let stand for a few minutes. Pour or skim off and discard any clear fat that rises to the surface. Add stock to the juices in the cup to make a total of 1½ cups (12 fl oz/375 ml).

● Place the pan over high heat. Add 1 tablespoon of the cold butter and the shallot and sauté until softened, about 1 minute. Pour in the stock mixture, scraping up the browned bits. Boil until reduced by half, about 5 minutes. Remove from the heat and whisk in the remaining 1 tablespoon cold butter. Season to taste. Carve the bird and serve right away on warmed plates. Pass the sauce at the table.

Canola oil

1 chicken, about
4 lb (2 kg)

4 tbsp (2 oz/60 g)
unsalted butter, 2 tbsp
at room temperature
and 2 tbsp cold

Kosher salt and freshly
ground pepper

2 sprigs fresh rosemary

About 1½ cups
(12 fl oz/375 ml)
Chicken Stock (page
138) or low-sodium
chicken broth

1 shallot, minced

MAKES 4 SERVINGS

A marinated whole chicken emerges wonderfully moist from the oven. This hearty wine-based marinade needs only 1 hour to infuse the chicken with savory flavor.

Marinated Roast Chicken

In a large glass bowl, mix together the wine, olive oil, mustard, garlic, herbes de Provence, ¼ teaspoon salt, and the red pepper flakes. Add the chicken and turn to coat well. Let stand at room temperature for 1 hour, turning occasionally.

Preheat the oven to 450°F (230°C). Remove the chicken from the marinade and drain well. Discard the marinade. Place the chicken on its back on an oiled V-shaped roasting rack in a flameproof roasting pan. Roast the bird for 15 minutes. Turn the chicken onto one of its sides, reduce the oven temperature to 375°F (190°C) and roast until an instant-read thermometer inserted into the thickest part of the thigh, not touching bone, reads 170°F (77°C), about 60 minutes longer, turning the bird on its other side halfway through. Transfer the chicken, breast side up, to a carving board and let rest for 10–20 minutes.

Pour the drippings from the pan into a 2-cup (16–fl oz/500-ml) glass measuring cup. Let stand for a few minutes and skim off and discard any clear fat that rises to the surface. Add stock to the juices to make a total of 1½ cups (12 fl oz/375 ml).

Place the pan over high heat. Add 1 tablespoon of the cold butter and the shallot and sauté until softened, about 1 minute. Pour in the stock mixture, scraping up the browned bits. Boil until reduced by half, about 5 minutes. Remove from the heat and whisk in the remaining 1 tablespoon cold butter. Season to taste. Carve the bird and serve right away on warmed plates. Pass the sauce at the table.

¾ cup (6 fl oz/180 ml) dry white wine

¼ cup (2 fl oz/60 ml) extra-virgin olive oil

1 tbsp Dijon mustard

2 cloves garlic, crushed

1 tbsp dried herbes de Provence

Kosher salt

¼ tsp red pepper flakes

1 chicken, about 4 lb (2 kg)

1½ cups (12 fl oz/ 375 ml) Chicken Stock (page 138) or low-sodium chicken broth

2 tbsp cold unsalted butter

1 shallot, minced

MAKES 4 SERVINGS

Instead of a light pan sauce, here's an old-fashioned gravy that would be tasty spooned over mashed sweet potatoes. Fruit cider sweetens as it reduces, complementing savory roast chicken.

Chicken with Cider Gravy

Canola oil

1 chicken, about
4 lb (2 kg)

4 tbsp (2 oz/60 g)
unsalted butter

Kosher salt and freshly
ground pepper

2 sprigs fresh rosemary

About ½ cup (4 fl oz/
125 ml) Chicken Stock
(page 138) or low-
sodium chicken broth

¾ cup hard apple or
pear cider

2 tbsp all-purpose flour

MAKES 4 SERVINGS

● Preheat the oven to 450°F (230°C). Brush a V-shaped rack with oil and place in a flameproof roasting pan.

● Pat dry the chicken, then rub with 2 tablespoons of the butter. Sprinkle with ¾ teaspoon salt and ½ teaspoon pepper. Slip the rosemary into the cavity. Tuck each wing behind the shoulders of the bird and place on its back on the oiled rack.

● Roast the bird for 15 minutes. Turn the chicken onto one of its sides, reduce the oven temperature to 375°F (190°C) and roast until an instant-read thermometer inserted into the thickest part of the thigh, not touching bone, reads 170°F (77°C), about 60 minutes longer, turning the bird on its other side halfway through. Transfer the chicken, breast side up, to a carving board and let rest for 10–20 minutes.

● Pour the drippings from the pan into a 2-cup (16–fl oz/500-ml) heatproof glass measuring cup. Let stand for a few minutes and skim off and discard any clear fat that rises to the surface. Add stock to the juices to make a total of ¾ cup (6 fl oz/ 180 ml), then add the cider. Melt the remaining 2 tablespoons butter in the pan over medium-low heat. Thoroughly whisk in the flour and let bubble without browning for 1 minute. Whisk in the cider mixture and bring to a simmer over medium-high heat. Reduce the heat to medium-low and cook until lightly thickened, about 5 minutes. Season to taste. Carve the bird and serve right away on warmed plates. Pass the gravy at the table.

Poultry has an affinity for fruity flavors, as shown in this simple recipe for small Cornish hens. It's a great, easy dish to serve to company because the individual hens make an elegant presentation.

Cornish Hens with Oranges & Onions

4 oranges

4 Cornish hens, about 1½ lb (750 g) each

4 cloves garlic, halved

Extra-virgin olive oil

Kosher salt and freshly ground pepper

4 sweet onions, thinly sliced

MAKES 6 SERVINGS

● Using a vegetable peeler, remove the zest from 1 of the oranges in ½-inch (12-mm) strips. Reserve the orange. Pat dry the hens. Place the zest strips and garlic in the cavities of the hens, dividing evenly. Brush the hens with oil, season lightly with salt and pepper, and cover and refrigerate for about 3 hours. Remove from the refrigerator 30 minutes before roasting.

● Preheat the oven to 425°F (220°C). Working with one orange at a time, cut a thin slice from the top and bottom of the fruit to expose the flesh. Stand the orange on a flat end, and, following the contour of the fruit, cut away all the peel and white pith all around the fruit. Working over a bowl, make a cut on both sides of each segment to free it from the membrane, letting the segment and juice drop into the bowl. Once all the fruits are segmented, coarsely chop the flesh.

● Add the onions to the bowl with the orange pieces and toss with 1½ tablespoons oil. Pour into a baking dish just large enough to hold the hens and spread out evenly. Place the hens, breast side up, on top of the onion-orange mixture. Roast until an instant-read thermometer inserted into the thickest part of the hen, not touching bone, registers 160°F (70°C), 50–60 minutes.

● Transfer the Cornish hens to a platter and let rest for 10 minutes. Divide the onion-orange mixture evenly among warmed individual plates, top each with a Cornish hen, and serve right away.

Fresh herbs, mixed into butter and spread under the skin, will not scorch as they do when sprinkled on the surface of the bird. The savory mixture also helps keep the breast meat moist.

Herb-Roasted Chicken

- Preheat the oven to 450°F (230°C). Brush a V-shaped roasting rack with oil and place in a roasting pan.

- In a bowl, mix together 2 tablespoons of the butter, the thyme, and rosemary.

- Pat dry the chicken. Carefully slip your fingers under the skin and work them all around the breast and thigh areas, loosening the skin. Using your fingers, evenly distribute the herb butter under the loosened skin (page 123).

- Rub the outside of the chicken with the remaining 2 tablespoons butter and sprinkle inside and out with ¾ teaspoon salt and ¼ teaspoon pepper. Place the bird on its back on the oiled rack.

- Roast the bird for 15 minutes. Turn the chicken onto one of its sides, reduce the oven temperature to 375°F (190°C) and roast until an instant-read thermometer inserted into the thickest part of the thigh, not touching bone, reads 170°F (77°C), about 60 minutes longer, turning the bird on its other side halfway through. Transfer the bird, breast side up, to a carving board and let rest for 10–20 minutes. Carve the chicken and serve right away on warmed plates.

Canola oil

4 tbsp (2 oz/60 g) unsalted butter, at room temperature

1 tsp chopped fresh thyme

1 tsp chopped fresh rosemary

1 chicken, about 4 lb (2 kg)

Kosher salt and freshly ground pepper

MAKES 4 SERVINGS

Honey and lemon zest add sweet and tart touches to roast chicken. Use your favorite flavored honey in this glaze. Either floral or herbal varieties will complement the sweet citrus tone in this dish.

Lemon & Honey Glazed Chicken

Canola oil

1 chicken, about
4 lb (2 kg)

4 tbsp (2 oz/60 g)
unsalted butter, 2 tbsp
at room temperature
and 2 tbsp cold

Kosher salt and freshly
ground pepper

2 sprigs fresh rosemary

2 tbsp lavender honey
or other full-flavored
honey

Grated zest of 1 large
lemon

MAKES 4 SERVINGS

● Preheat the oven to 450°F (230°C). Brush a V-shaped roasting rack with oil and place in a roasting pan.

● Pat dry the chicken, then rub evenly with the room-temperature butter. Sprinkle evenly with ¾ teaspoon salt and ½ teaspoon pepper. Slip the rosemary into the cavity. Tuck each wing behind the shoulders of the bird and place on its back on the oiled rack.

● Roast the bird for 15 minutes. Meanwhile, in a small bowl, mix together the honey and lemon zest.

● Turn the chicken onto one of its sides, reduce the oven temperature to 375°F (190°C) and roast for 30 minutes. Turn the chicken onto its other side and roast for 20 minutes. Turn the chicken breast-side up and brush the honey mixture all over the exposed surface. Return the chicken to the oven and roast until the glaze has thickened into a sheen and an instant-read thermometer inserted into the thickest part of the thigh, not touching bone, reads 170°F (77°C), about 10 minutes longer. Transfer the chicken, breast side up, to a carving board and let rest for 10–20 minutes. Carve the bird and serve right away on warmed plates.

A butterflied chicken roasts more quickly than an intact bird, with a particularly crisp finish. Mustard flavors both the glaze and the pan sauce, with a touch of cream to mellow the heat.

Honey-Mustard Chicken

- Preheat the oven to 425°F (220°C). Sprinkle both sides of the chicken with ¾ teaspoon salt and ¼ teaspoon pepper.

- Place the chicken, skin side up, on a large, heavy rimmed baking sheet. Roast until an instant-read thermometer inserted in the thickest part of the thigh, not touching bone, reads 155°F (68°C), about 35 minutes.

- Meanwhile, in a small bowl, stir together 2 tablespoons of the Dijon and the whole-grain mustards, honey, tarragon, and garlic. When the chicken reaches 155°F, remove it from the oven. Using the back of a spoon, spread the glaze all over the chicken skin. Return the chicken to the oven, and cook until the glaze has reduced to a shiny coating and an instant-read thermometer inserted in the thigh, not touching bone, reads 170°F (77°C), 10–15 minutes.

- Transfer the chicken to a platter and let stand, uncovered. Pour out and discard the drippings from the baking sheet, leaving any browned bits. Place the baking sheet on the stove top over high heat. When the pan begins to sizzle, add the stock, bring to a boil, and scrape up the browned bits. Boil until reduced by half, about 5 minutes. Whisk in the cream and remaining 1 tablespoon Dijon mustard and boil until lightly thickened, about 3 minutes longer. Season to taste.

- Cut the chicken in half lengthwise. Cut each half crosswise to create quarters. Serve right away on warmed plates. Pass the sauce at the table.

1 chicken, about 4 lb (2 kg), butterflied (page 121)

Kosher salt and freshly ground pepper

3 tbsp Dijon mustard

1 tbsp whole-grain mustard

1 tbsp thyme honey or other full-flavored honey

2 tsp finely chopped fresh tarragon

1 large clove garlic, minced

1¼ cups (10 fl oz/ 310 ml) Chicken Stock (page 138) or low-sodium chicken broth

3 tbsp heavy cream

MAKES 4 SERVINGS

Sweet potatoes, apple cider, and fresh sage are typical autumn ingredients. Here they combine with chicken pieces to create a simple baked main course, perfect for the fall months.

Chicken with Sweet Potatoes & Sage

- Preheat the oven to 375°F (190°C). Butter a large baking dish that will hold the chicken and potatoes in a single layer.

- In a frying pan over medium-high heat, melt 2 tablespoons of the butter with the oil. In 2 batches, cook the chicken until golden, 4–5 minutes per side. Transfer to the prepared dish. Arrange the sweet potato slices among the chicken pieces.

- Reduce the heat to medium-low and add the shallots. Sauté until translucent, 2–3 minutes. Add ¼ cup (2 fl oz/60 ml) each of the apple juice and stock and stir, scraping up any browned bits. Bring to a boil and pour into the dish. Tuck the sage leaves around the chicken and sprinkle lightly with salt and pepper.

- Bake until the potatoes are tender, the chicken is opaque throughout, and the juices run clear when pierced with a knife tip, 45–50 minutes. Transfer the chicken and potatoes to a warmed serving dish and cover to keep warm. Using a large spoon, skim off the fat from the pan juices and pour the juices into a glass measuring cup.

- In a small saucepan over medium-low heat, melt the remaining 1 tablespoon butter. Stir in the flour and cook until bubbly, 1–2 minutes. Raise the heat to medium. Stirring constantly, gradually add the remaining ¼ cup (2 fl oz/60 ml) each apple juice and stock and the pan juices until the mixture thickens and comes to a boil, 3–4 minutes. Add the cream and cook for a few seconds. Adjust the seasonings. Pour the sauce over the chicken and potatoes and serve right away.

3 tbsp unsalted butter, plus extra for greasing

2 tbsp vegetable oil

1 chicken, about 3½ lb (1.75 kg), cut into 8 pieces

2 lb (1 kg) sweet potatoes, peeled and sliced

8 shallots, thinly sliced

½ cup (4 fl oz/125 ml) apple juice

½ cup (4 fl oz/125 ml) Chicken Stock (page 138) or low-sodium chicken broth

6–8 fresh sage leaves

Kosher salt and freshly ground pepper

1 tbsp all-purpose flour

¼ cup (2 fl oz/60 ml) heavy cream

MAKES 4 SERVINGS

Red, green, and yellow bell peppers are a sweet match for chicken in this colorful main course. Make this simple dish in summer or early fall when bell peppers are piled high in the market.

Chicken & Sweet Peppers

6 tbsp (2¼ oz/67 g) all-purpose flour

4 *each* chicken breast halves, thighs, and drumsticks, skinned

2 tbsp olive oil

Kosher salt and freshly ground pepper

1 yellow onion, sliced

½ *each* red, green, and yellow bell pepper, sliced crosswise

2 cloves garlic, minced

1 tbsp *each* minced fresh basil, oregano, and flat-leaf parsley

3 cups (18 oz/560 g) peeled, seeded, and chopped tomatoes

1 cup (8 fl oz/250 ml) low-sodium chicken broth

½ cup (4 fl oz/125 ml) dry white wine

MAKES 8 SERVINGS

● Preheat the oven to 350°F (180°C). Spread the flour on a plate, then lightly coat both sides of each chicken piece with the flour, shaking off the excess.

● In a frying pan over high heat, warm the olive oil. In batches, add the chicken pieces and cook, turning once, until lightly browned, about 4 minutes total. Transfer to a baking dish large enough to hold all the chicken in a single layer. Season the chicken pieces lightly with salt and pepper.

● Reduce the heat to medium and add the onion, peppers, garlic, basil, oregano, and parsley. Sauté until the vegetables are softened, about 5 minutes. Stir in the tomatoes, broth, and wine, raise the heat to high, and bring to a boil. Pour the mixture evenly over the chicken in the dish.

● Cover with aluminum foil and bake until the chicken is opaque throughout and the juices run clear when pierced with a knife tip, 20–30 minutes. Serve right away directly from the dish.

Here, the classic Asian mixture of sweet, salty, and spicy flavors is achieved with hoisin sauce, soy sauce, and ginger. This recipe takes some planning, but the reward is succulent meat and crisp skin.

Duck with Hoisin Glaze

1 Muscovy or Long Island duck, about 5 lb, (2.5 kg), excess fat removed

2 qt (2 l) boiling water

Canola oil

½ inch (12 mm) slice fresh ginger, coarsely chopped

2 cloves garlic, coarsely chopped

1 green onion, white and tender green parts, coarsely chopped

1 tbsp soy sauce

¼ tsp red pepper flakes

1 cup (8 fl oz/250 ml) hot water

3 tbsp hoisin sauce

2 tbsp Chinese rice wine or dry sherry

MAKES 3–4 SERVINGS

● Place the duck, breast side up, on a flat rack in the sink. Slowly pour 2 cups (16 fl oz/500 ml) of the boiling water over the duck. Let stand for 2 minutes and repeat the process. Turn the duck over and repeat the procedure twice. Pat dry with paper towels. Place the duck on a flat wire rack set on a rimmed baking sheet and refrigerate uncovered for 18–24 hours.

● Preheat the oven to 400°F (200°C). Brush a V-shaped roasting rack with oil and place in a roasting pan. Rub the ginger, garlic, green onion, soy sauce, and red pepper flakes evenly in the duck cavity. Place the duck, breast side up, on the rack. Pour the hot water into the pan and roast the duck, without basting, until the skin is brown and crisp and an instant-read thermometer inserted into the thigh, away from bone, reads 170°–175°F (77°–80°C), about 1¼ hours. Every 15 minutes, use a bulb baster to remove the liquid from the pan. Transfer to a platter and let cool for 1–2 hours.

● Preheat the broiler. In a bowl, stir together the hoisin and wine. Cut the duck in half lengthwise. Cut each duck half crosswise to create quarters and place on the rack of a broiler pan. Broil until the skin is sizzling, about 1–2 minutes. Brush the hoisin mixture over the duck and broil until bubbling, about 1 minute longer. Transfer to warmed plates and serve right away.

Traditionally, chicken parmigiana is breaded and fried. Here is a lighter and simpler rendition, with chicken breasts browned on the stove top and finished in the oven with marinara and mozzarella.

Baked Chicken Parmesan

● Preheat the oven to 400°F (200°C). Season the chicken generously on all sides with salt and pepper.

● In a large ovenproof frying pan over medium-high heat, warm the oil. Add the chicken and cook, turning once, until golden brown, about 7 minutes total. Transfer to a plate and set aside.

● Add the kale to the pan and sauté over medium-high heat until wilted, about 1 minute. Return the chicken to the frying pan with the kale and pour over the marinara sauce. Place 2 cheese slices on each chicken breast. Sprinkle evenly with the Parmesan cheese. Bake until the cheese is golden and the chicken is opaque throughout, about 20 minutes. Serve right away on warmed plates.

4 boneless, skinless chicken breast halves, about 1½ lb (750 g) total weight

Kosher salt and freshly ground pepper

2 tbsp olive oil

1 bunch kale, leaves stripped from stems and torn into large pieces

2 cups (16 fl oz/500 ml) purchased marinara sauce, warmed

8 slices fresh mozzarella cheese, ¼ inch (6 mm) thick

½ cup (2 oz/60 g) freshly grated Parmesan cheese

MAKES 4 SERVINGS

Enchiladas are a delicious and imaginative way to enjoy chicken and vegetables, whether they are fresh or leftovers. This recipe uses tart tomatillo salsa, but you can also use a red chile sauce.

Layered Chicken Enchiladas

15 corn tortillas, halved

2 tbsp canola oil

Kosher salt

4 cups (1½ lb/750 g) shredded cooked chicken

2 cups (8 oz/250 g) shredded white Cheddar cheese

2 cups (12 oz/370 g) fresh or frozen corn kernels

2 zucchini, halved lengthwise and thinly sliced

1 large yellow onion, thinly sliced

2 jars (12½ oz/ 390 g each) purchased tomatillo salsa

¼ cup (2 oz/60 g) sour cream

½ cup (2½ oz/75 g) crumbled queso fresco

MAKES 4–6 SERVINGS

• Preheat the oven to 400°F (200°C). Brush the tortillas with the oil, sprinkle lightly with salt, and arrange on a baking sheet. Bake until crisp, 3–4 minutes. Remove from the oven and reduce the oven temperature to 300°F (150°C).

• In a small bowl, stir together the chicken, Cheddar cheese, corn, zucchini, and onion.

• Reserve one-fourth of the salsa for serving. Cover the bottom of a 9-inch (23-cm) round baking dish with a thin layer of salsa. Lay 10 tortilla halves over the salsa, overlapping if necessary. Top with one-fourth of the remaining salsa and one-third of the chicken-cheese mixture, spreading them evenly. Repeat the layers two more times. Top the final layer of chicken-cheese mixture with the remaining salsa. Spoon the sour cream evenly over the top, then sprinkle with the queso fresco.

• Cover the dish with aluminum foil and bake until the vegetables are tender and the cheese has melted, about 20 minutes. Uncover and continue to bake until the cheese is golden, 10–15 minutes longer. Let stand briefly before serving. Pass the reserved salsa at the table.

This refreshing salad is even easier to make with leftover cooked chicken and purchased shredded carrots. Use dried rice vermicelli or bean thread noodles; the latter will turn translucent when cooked.

Asian Chicken Salad

- Preheat the oven to 375°F (190°C). Place the chicken in a single layer on a rimmed baking sheet and cover with aluminum foil. Bake until opaque throughout, about 15 minutes. Remove from the oven and let cool. When cool enough to handle, cut the meat into bite-sized shreds.

- In a bowl, stir together the mint, ginger, garlic, jalapeño, soy sauce, lime juice, honey, and sesame oil.

- Remove 8 of the outer leaves from the cabbage head and reserve. Cut out the core and finely shred the remaining leaves; you should have about 4 cups (12 oz/375 g).

- Bring a large saucepan three-fourths full of water to a boil. Add the noodles and cook until tender, about 4 minutes. Drain and rinse under cold running water. Drain again and cut into 2-inch (5-cm) lengths.

- In a large bowl, combine the shredded cabbage, chicken, cucumbers, carrots, green onions, noodles, and soy sauce mixture. Let stand for 20 minutes to allow the flavors to blend.

- Line serving plates with the reserved cabbage leaves. Mound the salad in the center and serve right away.

1 lb (500 g) boneless, skinless chicken breast halves

⅓ cup (½ oz/15 g) chopped fresh mint

¼ cup (1¼ oz/37 g) minced fresh ginger

3 cloves garlic, minced

1 jalapeño, minced

¼ cup (2 fl oz/60 ml) soy sauce

3 tbsp *each* lime juice and honey

2 tsp Asian sesame oil

1 head napa cabbage, about 1¼ lb (625 g)

3 oz (90 g) dried rice vermicelli

2 cucumbers, peeled, seeded, and diced

2 cups (10 oz/310 g) shredded carrots

6 green onions, minced

MAKES 4 SERVINGS

Assemble this dish, put it in the oven, and forget the fuss—it is the quintessential one-pot meal. The tender chicken and vegetables baked in a flaky, buttery crust will please adults and children alike.

Skillet Chicken Potpie

● Preheat the oven to 375°F (190°C). In a large ovenproof frying pan over medium-high heat, melt 4 tablespoons of the butter. Add the leeks, season lightly with salt and pepper, and sauté until softened, about 5 minutes. Add the ⅓ cup (2 oz/60 g) flour and cook, stirring, for 2 minutes. Stir in the wine and broth and bring to a boil. Reduce the heat to low and simmer, stirring occasionally, until the liquid thickens slightly, about 5 minutes. Stir in the chicken and peas. Taste and adjust the seasonings with salt and pepper.

● In a large bowl, combine the 2 cups (10 oz/315 g) flour, the baking powder, and ½ teaspoon salt. Using a pastry blender or 2 knives, cut in the remaining 5 tablespoons (2½ oz/75 g) butter until the mixture forms coarse crumbs about the size of peas. Add the milk and, using a rubber spatula, stir until evenly moistened. Place heaping spoonfuls of the batter evenly over the chicken filling. Bake until the topping is golden brown and the filling is bubbling, about 25 minutes. Let stand for a few minutes before serving.

9 tbsp (4½ oz/140 g) cold unsalted butter

2 large leeks, white and pale green parts only, thinly sliced

Kosher salt and freshly ground pepper

⅓ cup (2 oz/60 g) plus 2 cups (10 oz/ 315 g) all-purpose flour

¼ cup (2 fl oz/60 ml) dry white wine

4 cups (32 fl oz/1 l) low-sodium chicken broth

About 4 cups (1½ lb/ 750 g) shredded cooked chicken meat

1 cup (5 oz/155 g) peas

4 tsp baking powder

1½ cups (12 fl oz/ 375 ml) milk

MAKES 4–6 SERVINGS

Goat cheese and olives pair for a simple but elegant sandwich, easy to pack and enjoy at a picnic. On a busy weekend, pick up roast chicken and tapenade at the store and assembly is a breeze.

Roast Chicken Sandwich

1 baguette, 24 inches (60 cm) long and 2½ inches (6 cm) in diameter

3 tbsp extra-virgin olive oil

1 large clove garlic, halved

¼ lb (125 g) creamy fresh goat cheese

¼ cup (2 oz/60 g) Tapenade (page 138 or purchased)

One 2½–3 lb (1.25–1.5 kg) roasted chicken, skin removed and meat sliced

3 plum tomatoes, sliced

Leaves from 1 small bunch fresh basil

Freshly ground pepper

MAKES 4 SERVINGS

● Place the baguette on a work surface and cut on the diagonal into 4 equal pieces. Cut each piece in half horizontally. Brush the cut surfaces with the olive oil.

● Place a stove-top grill pan over medium heat. When hot, place the bread, cut sides down, on the pan and grill until lightly browned, about 1 minute. Remove from the pan and rub the cut surfaces with the cut sides of the garlic clove.

● Spread the 4 bottom pieces of bread with the goat cheese, dividing evenly. Spread a thin layer of the Tapenade over the cheese. Place the sliced chicken over the Tapenade, and top with the tomato slices and several fresh basil leaves. Grind some fresh pepper over the top. Close the sandwiches and serve right away.

Simmering and braising are two related cooking methods that cook food partially or fully covered with gently simmering liquid for a relatively long period of time in an enclosed cooking vessel. These methods promote tenderness and create concentrated

Simmered & Braised

flavors, often incorporating the cooking liquid as part of the finished dish. Simmering and braising are used for making some of the most beloved dishes—a nourishing chicken soup, an exotically spiced stew, a home-style pasta, or a southern-style one-pot meal. The recipes that follow offer plenty of inspiration for any meal.

Cuts for Simmering/Braising

Braised recipes usually call for pieces of poultry. Many recipes use only breasts and thighs, others include the whole cut-up bird. Bone-in cuts are best, as they provide the most flavor. Some simmered recipes use a whole bird, which is then removed from the liquid, the meat pulled from the bones, and returned to the cooking liquid.

Choosing Pots

The best braising pot is the timeless Dutch oven with its tight-fitting lid. A heavy, deep-sided frying pan with a lid is also useful. In either case, enameled cast iron is best, as it holds heat well, and boasts a stick-resistant surface. Heavy stainless steel, aluminum-clad stainless steel, or anodized aluminum pots are fine alternatives.

Browning Chicken

Browning chicken or vegetables in oil before braising or simmering in liquid caramelizes the natural sugars, developing rich surface color and deep flavor. Do not skip this step. Resist the temptation to lift pieces up every few seconds—doing so interferes with the process and can lead to a loss of moisture and sticking.

Tips & Tricks

Flambéing Safety

When flambéing, always transfer the brandy, or other liquor, from its original bottle to another container before adding it to the pan. The flame can travel into the bottle and cause it to burst. Additionally, remove the pan from the heat when pouring in the liquor, especially if using a gas stove. Keep pot holders or towels well out of reach of the flames.

Reducing Liquids

An important step in simmering and braising is reducing the cooking liquid. This typically involves simmering the liquid briskly for several minutes, reducing its volume, concentrating its flavor, and thickening its body. This process will also evaporate some of the alcohol content of wine or spirits, eliminating their sometimes-harsh edge and bringing out the flavor.

Using Leftovers

One of the biggest benefits of braising and simmering is that dishes often taste better the next day, which is a boon to the busy cook. Cool the dish to room temperature, transfer it to an airtight container, then label clearly with the contents and date. Rewarm dishes over medium-low heat until thoroughly heated through before serving. Use within 3 or 4 days.

In this timeless French recipe, chicken is simmered with robust red wine, earthy mushrooms, and salty bacon. Serve with steamed potatoes or egg noodles and garnish with fresh parsley, if desired.

Coq au Vin

- Season the chicken with 1 teaspoon salt and ½ teaspoon pepper. Cut the pancetta into small strips.

- Preheat the oven to 325°F (165°C). In a large Dutch oven over medium-high heat, heat 1 tablespoon of the oil. Add the pancetta and lightly brown, about 6 minutes. Drain on paper towels. Pour out all but 1 tablespoon fat.

- Return the pot to medium-high heat. Add the mushrooms and sauté until brown, about 8 minutes. Transfer to a plate. Add the remaining 2 tablespoons oil. In batches, cook the chicken until brown on all sides, about 6 minutes total. Transfer to a plate.

- Reduce the heat to medium-low, add the butter and shallots and sauté until softened, 2 minutes. Stir in the mushrooms. Off the heat, add the Cognac, then return to medium heat and use a long match to ignite it. Cook until the flames disappear and the Cognac has almost evaporated, about 1 minute.

- Stir in the flour. Add the wine, stock, thyme, tomato paste, and bay leaf and raise the heat to high. Bring to a boil, scraping up the browned bits. Return the drumsticks, thighs, wings, and breasts, in that order, to the pot. Cover tightly and bake until the chicken has no signs of pink at the bone when pierced with a knife, about 40 minutes. During the last 5 minutes, stir in the reserved pancetta.

- Transfer the chicken to a warmed deep platter. Skim the fat from the sauce, adjust the seasonings, and pour over the chicken. Serve right away.

1 chicken, 4 lb (2 kg), cut into 10 pieces

Kosher salt and freshly ground pepper

¼ lb (125 g) pancetta

3 tbsp canola oil

10 oz (315 g) cremini mushrooms, quartered

2 tbsp unsalted butter

2 shallots, minced

¼ cup (2 fl oz/60 ml) Cognac

¼ cup (1½ oz/45 g) all-purpose flour

1 cup (8 fl oz/250 ml) dry red wine

1 cup (8 fl oz/250 ml) Chicken Stock (page 138)

1 tsp fresh thyme

1 tsp tomato paste

½ bay leaf

MAKES 4 SERVINGS

Cacciatore means "woodsman's style," referring to the use of mushrooms in the sauce. Along with the earthy flavor of the fungi are hearty red wine, sweet-tart tomatoes, and woodsy herbs.

Chicken Cacciatore

● Season the chicken with 1 teaspoon salt and ½ teaspoon pepper.

● In a large Dutch oven over medium-high heat, heat the oil. In batches, cook the chicken until brown on all sides, about 6 minutes per batch. Transfer to a platter. Add the mushrooms and sauté until the mushrooms give off their juices, about 5 minutes. Add the onion and garlic and sauté until the mushrooms begin to brown, about 3 minutes. Add the tomatoes and their juice, the wine, rosemary, and sage.

● Return the drumsticks, thighs, wings, and breasts, in that order, to the pot and bring to a boil. Reduce the heat to medium-low, cover, and cook until the chicken shows no signs of pink at the bone when pierced with a knife, about 40 minutes.

● Transfer the chicken to a warmed deep platter. Skim the fat from the sauce, adjust the seasonings, and pour over the chicken. Serve right away.

1 chicken, about 4 lb (2 kg), cut into 10 pieces

Kosher salt and freshly ground pepper

1 tbsp extra-virgin olive oil

10 oz (315 g) cremini mushrooms, quartered

1 small onion, chopped

1 clove garlic, finely chopped

1 can (28 oz/875 g) diced tomatoes

½ cup (4 fl oz/125 ml) dry red wine

1 tsp dried rosemary

½ tsp dried sage

MAKES 4 SERVINGS

Garlic becomes sweet and mellow with long cooking, a wonderful transformation in slow-cooked dishes. Even a large amount of garlic, as in this recipe, will lose its intensity, creating a delicious sauce.

Braised Garlic Chicken

1 chicken, about 4 lb (2 kg), cut into 10 pieces

Kosher salt and freshly ground pepper

1 tbsp extra-virgin olive oil

40 garlic cloves, unpeeled

1/2 cup (4 fl oz/125 ml) dry white wine

1 cup (8 fl oz/250 ml) Chicken Stock (page 138)

1/2 tsp dried thyme

MAKES 4 SERVINGS

● Season the chicken with 1 teaspoon salt and 1/2 teaspoon pepper.

● In a large Dutch oven over medium-high heat, heat the oil. In batches, cook the chicken until brown on all sides, about 6 minutes per batch. Transfer to a platter. Add the garlic cloves and sauté for about 2 minutes, without browning. Add the wine, bring to a boil, and stir to scrape up the browned bits. Add the stock and thyme.

● Return the drumsticks, thighs, wings, and breasts, in that order, to the pot and bring to a boil. Reduce the heat to medium-low, cover, and cook until the chicken shows no signs of pink at the bone when pierced with a knife, about 40 minutes.

● Transfer the chicken to a warmed deep platter and cover with aluminum foil to keep warm. Skim the fat from the sauce and boil until reduced by one-fourth. Strain through a coarse-mesh sieve placed over a bowl, pressing the garlic flesh through the sieve with a spatula. Discard the garlic skins. Adjust the seasonings. Pour the sauce over the chicken and serve right away.

This dish features the sunny flavors of Provence. The chicken simmers in its own juices along with tangy tomatoes and a crisp white wine that together impart a delightfully tart quality.

Chicken with Tomatoes & Olives

1 chicken, about 4 lb (2 kg), cut into 10 pieces

Kosher salt and freshly ground black pepper

1 tbsp olive oil

2 shallots, minced

2 cloves garlic, chopped

½ cup (4 fl oz/125 ml) dry white wine

1 can (28 oz/875 g) diced tomatoes

2 tsp dried herbes de Provence

⅛ tsp red pepper flakes

½ cup (2½ oz/75 g) pitted Kalamata olives

1 tbsp chopped fresh rosemary or flat-leaf parsley

MAKES 4 SERVINGS

- Season the chicken with ½ teaspoon salt and ¼ teaspoon pepper.

- In a large Dutch oven over medium-high heat, heat the oil. In batches, cook the chicken until brown on all sides, about 6 minutes per batch. Transfer to a platter. Pour off all but 1 tablespoon fat. Return the pot to medium heat. Add the shallots and garlic and sauté until softened, about 2 minutes. Add the wine, bring to a boil, and stir to scrape up the browned bits. Stir in the tomatoes and their juice, the herbes de Provence, and the red pepper flakes.

- Return the drumsticks, thighs, wings, and breasts, in that order, to the pot and bring to a boil. Reduce the heat to medium-low, cover, and cook until the chicken shows no signs of pink at the bone when pierced with a knife, about 40 minutes.

- Transfer the chicken to a warmed platter and cover with aluminum foil to keep warm. Remove the sauce from the heat and let stand for 3 minutes. Skim the fat from the sauce and boil until reduced by about one-fourth, about 5 minutes. Add the olives and heat through, about 1 minute. Adjust the seasonings.

- Divide the chicken among warmed bowls and pour the sauce over the top. Sprinkle with the rosemary and serve right away.

Bone-in chicken infuses the most flavor in a stewpot, emerging succulent after braising. The flavors of Spain—smoky paprika, dry sherry, and bold green olives—combine in this hearty stew.

Spanish-Style Braised Chicken

• Season the chicken with ½ teaspoon salt and ¼ teaspoon pepper.

• In a large Dutch oven over medium-high heat, heat the oil. In batches, cook the chicken until brown on all sides, about 6 minutes per batch. Transfer to a platter. Add the onion, bell pepper, and garlic and sauté over medium heat until the onion has softened, about 5 minutes. Stir in the paprika and oregano. Add the sherry, bring to a boil, and stir to scrape up the browned bits. Stir in the diced tomatoes with their juice.

• Return the drumsticks, thighs, wings, and breasts, in that order, to the pot and bring to a boil. Reduce the heat to medium-low, cover, and cook until the chicken shows no signs of pink at the bone when pierced with a knife, about 40 minutes. During the last 5 minutes of cooking, add the green olives.

• Transfer the chicken to a warmed deep platter and cover with aluminum foil to keep warm. Skim the fat from the sauce and boil until reduced by one-fourth, about 5 minutes. Taste and adjust the seasonings. Pour the sauce over the chicken and serve right away.

1 chicken, about 4 lb (2 kg), cut into 10 pieces

Kosher salt and freshly ground pepper

1 tbsp extra-virgin olive oil

1 yellow onion, chopped

1 red bell pepper, diced

2 cloves garlic, minced

1 tbsp smoked Spanish paprika

½ tsp dried oregano

⅓ cup (3 fl oz/80 ml) dry sherry

1 can (28 oz/875 g) diced tomatoes

½ cup (2½ oz/75 g) coarsely chopped green olives

MAKES 4 SERVINGS

Fresh artichokes yield the best flavor in this dish. If they are unavailable, use about 1½ cups (12 oz/375 g) thawed, frozen hearts or drained, marinated hearts and add them with the tomatoes.

Braised Chicken & Artichokes

1 lemon, halved

1 lb (500 g) small artichokes

3 tbsp all-purpose flour

2 *each* chicken breast halves, thighs, and drumsticks, skinned

2 tbsp olive oil

Kosher salt and freshly ground pepper

4 cloves garlic, slivered

1 shallot, slivered

1 tbsp *each* minced fresh basil, tarragon, and flat-leaf parsley

1 tbsp Dijon mustard

1 cup (8 fl oz/250 ml) dry white wine

½ cup (4 fl oz/125 ml) Chicken Stock (page 138)

3 plum tomatoes, seeded and chopped

MAKES 4–6 SERVINGS

● Add the juice of ½ lemon to a large bowl of water. One at a time, cut off the artichoke stems at the base and cut off the top third. Snap off the tough outer leaves to reveal the pale inner leaves and trim any dark areas around the base. Rub the cut surfaces with the remaining lemon half. Halve the artichoke lengthwise and use a spoon to scoop out the prickly choke. Cut each half in half again and add to the lemon water.

● Spread the flour on a plate, then lightly coat the chicken with the flour, shaking off the excess. In a frying pan over medium-high heat, warm the oil. When hot, add the chicken and sauté, turning once, until lightly browned, 1–2 minutes on each side. Transfer to a platter, season with salt and pepper, and set aside.

● Pour out all but 2 tablespoons of fat from the pan. Add the garlic and shallot and sauté until softened, 1–2 minutes. Stir in the herbs and mustard. Add the wine and stock, and bring to a boil, scraping up the browned bits. Add the tomatoes.

● Return the thighs and drumsticks to the pot, reduce the heat to medium, and simmer for 10 minutes. Add the breasts and cook for 10 minutes more. Drain the artichokes, add to the pan, and cook until the chicken juices run clear when pierced and the artichokes are tender, about 10 minutes longer.

● Transfer to a warmed deep serving platter and serve right away.

Moroccan cooking seduces with deeply aromatic spices—here, fragrant cinnamon, cayenne, and saffron. Bitter green olives lend a nice counterpoint. If you like, garnish with chopped fresh cilantro.

Moroccan-Style Chicken

- Season the chicken with ¾ teaspoon salt and ¼ teaspoon pepper.

- In a large Dutch oven over medium-high heat, heat the oil. In batches, cook the chicken until brown on all sides, about 6 minutes per batch. Transfer to a platter.

- Pour off all but 2 tablespoons fat. Return the pot to medium heat. Add the onion and sauté until golden, about 10 minutes. Stir in the garlic and cook until fragrant, about 2 minutes. Add the ginger, paprika, cumin, coriander, cinnamon, and cayenne and sauté until fragrant, about 15 seconds.

- Return the chicken to the pot with the stock, saffron, and half of the lemon zest. Bring to a boil, reduce the heat to medium-low, and cover tightly. Cook until the chicken shows no sign of pink at the bone when pierced with a knife, about 40 minutes. During the last 5 minutes of cooking, stir in the olives and remaining half of the lemon zest.

- Transfer the chicken to a warmed serving bowl and cover with aluminum foil to keep warm. Remove the sauce from the heat and let stand for 3 minutes. Skim the fat from the sauce and adjust the seasonings. Pour the sauce over the chicken and serve right away.

4 whole chicken legs, about 2½ lb (1.25 kg) total weight

Kosher salt and freshly ground pepper

1 tbsp olive oil

1 large onion, diced

3 cloves garlic, minced

1 tsp ground ginger

2 tsp sweet paprika

1 tsp *each* ground cumin and coriander

¼ tsp ground cinnamon

⅛ tsp cayenne pepper

1½ cups (12 fl oz/ 375 ml) Chicken Stock (page 138)

4 tsp saffron threads

Grated zest of 1 lemon

24 large green olives, coarsely chopped

MAKES 4 SERVINGS

Enjoy this hearty stew on cold days. Butternut squash and mushrooms join a medley of vegetables, while hot Italian sausage packs heat, making the stew as warming as it is filling.

Chicken & Vegetable Stew

- Sprinkle the chicken evenly with the paprika.

- In a Dutch oven over high heat, heat the oil. In batches, cook the chicken, turning once, until browned, about 2 minutes on each side. Transfer to a plate and season with salt and pepper.

- Reduce the heat to medium and add the sausages. Cook until browned on all sides, about 4 minutes total. Transfer to a cutting board and, when cool enough to handle, slice into rounds ½ inch (12 mm) thick.

- Raise the heat to medium-high, add the carrots and onion, and sauté until the onion is softened, about 4 minutes. Stir in the flour for 1 minute. Add the stock and scrape up the browned bits. Add the wine, squash, potatoes, and thyme.

- Return the chicken and sausage to the pot, season with salt and pepper, and bring to a simmer. Add half of the mushrooms, reduce the heat to medium-low, cover partially, and simmer until the chicken juices run clear when pierced and the potatoes are tender, about 20 minutes. Stir in the remaining mushrooms and cook until tender, 5–10 minutes longer.

- Transfer to warmed individual serving bowls and serve right away.

4 *each* chicken breast halves, thighs, and drumsticks, skinned

1 tbsp sweet paprika

2 tbsp olive oil

Kosher salt and freshly ground pepper

½ lb (250 g) hot Italian sausages

10–12 baby carrots

1 onion, chopped

2 tbsp all-purpose flour

1½ cups (12 fl oz/ 375 ml) *each* Chicken Stock (page 138) and dry white wine

2 cups (10 oz/300 g) butternut squash cubes

10 small red potatoes

2 tsp dried thyme

½ lb (250 g) cremini mushrooms, sliced

MAKES 8 SERVINGS

Popular in Thai restaurants, this delicate and fragrant soup is easily prepared at home. Most of the Asian ingredients can be found in a well-stocked supermarket or an Asian grocery store.

Coconut Chicken Soup

3 large limes

4 cups (32 fl oz/1 l) Chicken Stock (page 138)

4 thin slices fresh ginger

1 large lemongrass stalk, cut into 2-inch (5-cm) pieces, crushed

2 cans (14 fl oz/430 ml each) coconut milk

2 tbsp Asian fish sauce

2 tbsp brown sugar

1 tbsp Thai red curry paste

1 lb (500 g) boneless, skinless chicken breasts

½ lb (250 g) white mushrooms, sliced

5 small fresh red chiles, thinly sliced

Fresh cilantro leaves

MAKES 4–6 SERVINGS

● Finely grate the zest from 1 of the limes and then squeeze the juice. Cut the remaining 2 limes into wedges.

● In a large saucepan, combine the stock, ginger, lemongrass, and lime zest. Place over medium heat and bring to a boil. Let boil for 1 minute.

● Reduce the heat to low, stir in the coconut milk, and bring to a simmer. Add the lime juice, fish sauce, brown sugar, and curry paste and mix well. Simmer for 5 minutes.

● Cut the chicken into bite-sized pieces, add to the pan, and simmer until opaque throughout, 4–5 minutes. Add the mushrooms and simmer until tender, about 1 minute longer.

● Divide the soup among warmed individual bowls. Float the chile slices and cilantro leaves on top and serve right away. Pass the lime wedges at the table.

A good chicken soup offers garden-fresh vegetables and tender chicken in a rich, clear, full-bodied stock. For the juiciest meat and richest stock, this recipe uses a whole brined chicken.

Chicken Noodle Soup

1 chicken, about 3½ lb (1.75 kg)

Kosher salt and freshly ground pepper

3 qt (3 l) Chicken Stock (page 138)

2 carrots, diced

2 stalks celery, diced

1 yellow onion, diced

¼ lb (125 g) wide egg noodles, broken into 1–2 inch (2.5–5 cm) lengths

Chopped fresh flat-leaf parsley for garnish, optional

MAKES 6 SERVINGS

● Place the chicken in an extra-large glass bowl and cover with cold water. Drain and repeat. Return the chicken to the bowl, sprinkle ¼ cup salt evenly over it, and add cold water to cover by at least 1 inch (2.5 cm). Let stand for about 30 minutes.

● Drain the chicken and place in a large, heavy pot with the stock. Slowly bring to a boil over medium-high heat. As soon as you see bubbles form, reduce the heat to low and simmer. During the first 10 minutes, use a large spoon to skim any foam on the surface. Cook until a chicken leg starts to separate from the body when prodded, about 1½ hours, skimming every 30 minutes or so.

● Transfer the chicken to a deep platter and let cool for about 20 minutes. Using a large metal spoon, carefully skim and discard the fat from the surface of the stock.

● Pull off and discard the chicken skin, then cut the meat from the bone. Shred the chicken meat into bite-sized pieces to yield 1½ cups (9 oz/280 g); reserve the rest of the chicken meat for another use.

● Add the carrots, celery, onion, noodles, and ½ teaspoon salt to the broth, place over medium-low heat, and bring to a simmer. Cover and cook for 10 minutes. Add the chicken and continue to cook until the vegetables are tender, about 5 minutes longer. Adjust the seasonings. Ladle into warmed bowls, garnish with the parsley, if using, and serve right away.

Here is a traditional American Sunday dinner that couldn't be easier to prepare. A potful of chicken and vegetables topped with plump dumplings is comfort food at its filling and scrumptious best.

Chicken & Dumplings

- Place the chicken, breast side up, in a Dutch oven. Add the celery, carrots, bell pepper, rutabaga, parsnip, onion, garlic, bay leaf, 2 teaspoons salt, ½ teaspoon pepper, and the thyme, distributing evenly. Add water just to cover the bird. Bring to a boil over high heat, then reduce the heat to medium-low, cover, and simmer until the chicken is opaque throughout and the vegetables are tender, about 50 minutes.

- In a bowl, stir together the flour, baking powder, and 2 teaspoons salt. Using a pastry blender or your fingers, work in the butter until the mixture resembles coarse crumbs. Add the parsley. Using a fork, stir in the milk until a firm dough forms. Pinch off pieces of dough and roll into 8–10 equal-sized balls.

- When the chicken is ready, transfer it to a platter and cover loosely with aluminum foil to keep warm.

- Raise the heat under the pot to medium-high. Bring the broth to a boil, skimming off any foam that rises to the surface. Using a slotted spoon, lower the dumplings into the boiling broth. Cover and cook until the dumplings puff and the interiors are uniformly set when a dumpling is cut into, 10–15 minutes.

- Carve the chicken into serving pieces and transfer to warmed individual bowls. Place 1 or 2 dumplings in each bowl. Ladle the vegetables and broth into the bowls and serve right away.

1 chicken, 3½–4 lb (1.75–2 kg)

2 *each* celery stalks and carrots, sliced

1 *each* green bell pepper, rutabaga, parsnip, and yellow onion, diced

3 cloves garlic, minced

1 bay leaf

Kosher salt and freshly ground pepper

1 tsp dried thyme

1 cup (5 oz/155 g) all-purpose flour

1½ tsp baking powder

3 tbsp cold unsalted butter

¼ cup (⅓ oz/10 g) minced fresh flat-leaf parsley

¼ cup (2 fl oz/60 ml) milk

MAKES 4–6 SERVINGS

The mixture of crumbled goat cheese, lemon zest, and herbs makes a particularly pleasing garnish for sweet, mellow onions and chicken. You can substitute 1 pound (500 g) dried pasta with excellent results.

Pasta with Chicken & Onion Sauce

2½ lb (1.25 kg) boneless, skinless chicken breasts

Olive oil

3 onions, thinly sliced

½ tsp sugar

1 tbsp minced garlic

3 tbsp all-purpose flour

3 tbsp minced fresh rosemary

Kosher salt and freshly ground pepper

3 cups (24 fl oz/ 750 ml) Chicken Stock (page 138)

1 cup (8 fl oz/250 ml) dry white wine

1¼ lb (625 g) fresh fettuccine

6 oz (185 g) goat cheese

1 tbsp grated lemon zest

MAKES 6 SERVINGS

● Cut the chicken into 1-inch (2.5 cm) cubes. In a large, heavy frying pan over medium heat, warm 2 tablespoons olive oil. Add the onions and sugar and sauté until the onions are limp and golden, about 15 minutes. Transfer to a plate.

● Add 2 tablespoons olive oil to the pot and place over medium-high heat. Working in batches, add the chicken in a single layer and cook until browned on all sides, 2–3 minutes. Transfer to a plate.

● Return all the browned chicken to the pot and place over medium-high heat. Add the garlic and sauté until fragrant, about 1 minute. Sprinkle in the flour and toss well. Stir in 2½ tablespoons of the rosemary, ½ teaspoon of salt, and ¼ teaspoon pepper. Stir in the broth, wine, and reserved onions and bring to a simmer. Reduce the heat to low and cook, uncovered, until the chicken is fork tender, about 45 minutes. Taste and adjust the seasonings.

● Just before the chicken is ready, bring a large pot three-fourths full of generously salted water to a boil. Add the pasta, stir well, and cook until al dente, about 3 minutes. Drain and return to the pot.

● Divide the pasta among warmed plates and ladle the chicken-onion mixture on top, dividing evenly. Sprinkle each serving with equal amounts of the goat cheese, lemon zest, and the remaining ½ tablespoon rosemary. Serve right away.

Cutting Up a Whole Chicken

1 Remove the legs
Place the chicken breast side up on a board. Pull a leg away from the body. Using poultry shears, cut through the skin to expose the hip joint, and cut it to remove the leg. Repeat with the second leg.

2 Separate the thighs
Locate the joint between the thigh and drumstick. Holding a leg securely, use the poultry shears to cut through the joint to separate the thigh from the drumstick. Repeat with the second leg.

3 Remove the wings
Grasp a wing and pull it away from the body. Use the shears to cut through the skin to expose the shoulder joint. Then cut through the joint to remove the wing. Repeat with the second wing.

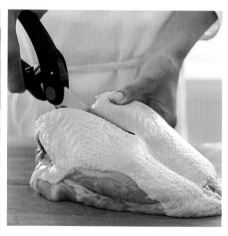

4 Remove the back
Turn the chicken over. Cut along one side of the backbone, from the body cavity to the neck cavity. Then cut along the other side and remove the back. Discard the back or save it for making stock.

5 Pull out the breastbone
Run the tip of the closed poultry shears through the membrane covering the breastbone. Bend the breast upward at the center to pop out the breastbone, then pull or cut it free and discard.

6 Cut the breast into halves
Cut the breast length-wise into 2 halves. After cutting up the chicken, you will have a total of 8 pieces plus the back. If the recipe calls for 10 pieces, cut the breast halves in half again crosswise.

Butterflying Chicken

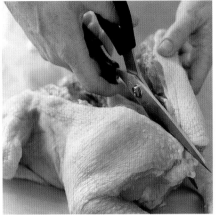

1 Cut along the backbone
Place the chicken, breast side down, on a cutting board. Using poultry shears or a chef's knife, cut along one side of the backbone. Pull open chicken, taking care not to rip or tear the skin.

2 Remove the backbone
Still using the knife or the shears, cut down along the other side of the backbone and remove the back. Discard the back or save it for making stock (see page 138).

3 Flatten the chicken
Turn the chicken breast side up on the board, opening the cavity. Placing one hand over the other, press firmly on the breast area to crack the breastbone and completely flatten the bird.

4 Secure the wings
Using your hands, bend each wing out from the body and secure the tip underneath the "shoulder" area. This will help the chicken to cook evenly and prevent the wing tips from burning.

Pounding a Chicken Breast

1 Remove the tenderloin
If necessary, grasp the skin and firmly pull it off the meat. Using a knife, cut away the long tenderloin and its white tendon from the breast. Reserve for another use.

2 Pound the breast half
Place 1 breast half in a plastic bag or between 2 sheets of waxed paper. Using a flat meat pounder, and working from the center outward, lightly pound the breast until it is a uniform ½ inch (12 mm) thick.

SKINNING & BONING CHICKEN BREAST HALVES

Boneless, skinless chicken breasts have become standard grocery items for the household cook, due to their convenience and the fact that they cook very quickly. Bone-in breasts, however, are a more economical buy, and are easy to bone at home, with just a few strokes of a sharp knife. Leftover bones can be reserved and used for stock, another benefit. It is equally easy to remove the skin from chicken breast halves, which removes about one-third of the fat.

First, remove the skin: If necessary, cut whole boneless chicken breasts into 2 halves. Working from the thick end of a breast half, grasp the skin and firmly pull it off the meat. Discard the skin. (To remove the skin from a drumstick, pull the skin from the meaty part down and off the drumstick, and cut to remove.)

Next, cut away the bones: Turn the chicken breast over. Starting from the thin end of the breast, and using a boning knife with a thin blade, cut the flesh away from the bone, using your other hand to pull the bone away as you cut. Discard the bones or reserve them for another use.

Finally, remove the tendon: Holding onto the end of the tough white tendon on the underside of the breast, scrape the meat away from it with a knife. Discard the tendon.

Skewering Boneless Breast Meat

1 Pound the breast meat
One at a time, place the chicken breast halves between 2 sheets of waxed paper or in a plastic bag. Using a meat pounder, gently pound the breast until the meat is equally thick throughout.

2 Cut the meat into cubes
Slice each breast half lengthwise into strips about 1 inch (2.5 cm) wide, or according to your recipe. Then, cut the strips crosswise into 1-inch (2.5-cm) square pieces, or as directed in the recipe.

3 Soak the skewers
Place bamboo skewers in a long, shallow dish and add cold water to cover. Let the skewers soak for at least 30 minutes to prevent the skewers from scorching during cooking. Drain before using.

4 Skewer the chicken
Thread 1 piece of chicken onto each soaked skewer, or more if called for in the recipe. Poke the skewer lengthwise through the center of each piece of meat so the pieces lie flat as they cook.

Trussing Poultry

1 Trim the fat

Trussing poultry is an optional step, but some believe it gives the bird a more pleasing, uniform appearance when cooked. Place the bird breast side up on a clean cutting board. Using poultry shears, cut off and discard any excess fat.

2 Secure the wings

Holding a wing tip with your hand, pull it out and then bend it to secure it underneath the "shoulder" area. This process will help the chicken to cook evenly and prevent the wing tips from burning in the high heat of the oven. Repeat to secure the other wing.

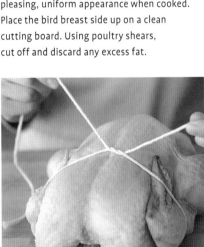

3 Or, tie the wings to the body

Instead of positioning the wings underneath the body, you can also secure the wings to the bird with a length of kitchen string. Don't tie the string too tightly or it could mar the skin.

4 Tie the drumsticks

Cut a length of kitchen string, loop it around the ends of the drumsticks, and tie the string in a secure knot to hold them in place. Snip the strings with kitchen shears just before carving.

Rubbing Butter Under the Skin

1 Separate the skin from the flesh

With the bird breast side up on a cutting board, slide your fingers under the skin and gently separate the skin from the breast meat on both sides. Take care not to tear the skin. Repeat under the skin of the leg and thigh areas.

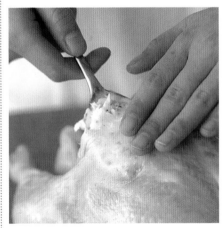

2 Rub the butter under the skin

Using a large spoon, scoop up a portion of flavored butter, slide it under the breast, leg, and thigh skin, and push it off with your fingers. Massage the butter into the flesh through the skin to distribute it evenly.

Brining Poultry

1 Dissolve the salt and sugar
Brining poultry before cooking enhances flavor and moistness. In a large saucepan, combine the brine ingredients. Bring to a boil over high heat, stirring often to dissolve the salt and sugar.

2 Transfer to a large vessel
Pour the brine into a large nonreactive pot or heatproof bowl large enough to hold the ingredients. Choose a vessel made from glass, ceramic, stainless steel, or plastic. Do not use uncoated aluminum.

3 Cool the brine
It is important for the brine to be cool before adding the poultry. Some recipes will call for a minimum of liquid in step 1 so that the solution can be diluted with ice water to cool it quickly.

  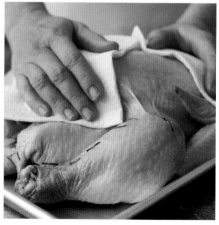

4 Add the bird to the brine
Add the poultry to the brining vessel, placing a plate on top of it to keep it completely submerged in the chilled brine. Refrigerate, turning occasionally, for 4–6 hours, or according to your recipe.

5 Drain the poultry
Remove the bird from the brine. If using a whole bird, place it in a large bowl, with the body cavity opening facing down, and let the it drain well for about 5 minutes to remove any remaining brine in the cavity.

6 Pat the bird dry
Some recipes call for rinsing the poultry before cooking to remove some of the salty flavor left by the brine. Before cooking, pat the bird completely dry and bring it to room temperature.

Sautéing Boneless Breasts

1 Heat the butter and oil
Choose a frying pan large enough to hold the chicken breasts without crowding. Place the frying pan over medium-high heat and add butter and/or oil to form a thin layer in the bottom of the pan.

2 Coat the breasts with flour
Spread flour in a shallow dish. One at a time, lightly coat seasoned, pounded, skinless chicken breasts (see page 121) in the flour, shaking off any excess, and place the coated breasts in the hot pan.

3 Sauté the chicken breasts
Let the breasts cook in the hot fat, without disturbing them, until the undersides are golden brown and crisp, about 3 minutes. Using tongs or an offset spatula, turn over the breasts to cook the other side.

4 Test for doneness
Reduce the heat to medium and cook until the second sides are golden brown and the breasts feel firm when pressed in the center with a fingertip (see page 135), about 3 minutes longer.

PAN TYPES

When it comes to choosing pans for sautéing, there are many choices to make. True sauté pans have high, angled handles and relatively high sides to help prevent food from bouncing out of the pan when it is being stirred. Slope-sided frying pans also work well for sautéing.

Stainless steel A favored material because of its durability, beauty, and the fact that it is dishwasher safe, stainless steel does not corrode or react with acidic ingredients, and is relatively resistant to sticking. High-quality pans will feature aluminum cores to encourage even heat distribution.

Cast-Iron Slow heating, cast iron retains and distributes heat very well. An uncoated cast-iron pan is the ideal choice for pan sauces, as it allows flavorful brown bits to adhere to the bottom. Uncoated pans do require seasoning: rubbing the interior with a small amount of cooking oil after hand-washing and drying. Enamel-coated cast-iron is slightly more stick-resistant, and does not react with acidic foods or impart metallic flavors. Enamels come in a rainbow of stylish colors.

Nonstick surfaces Prized because they release food quickly and easily to yield attractive results and quick and easy cleanup, nonstick surfaces also require little if any fat. They are especially helpful in low-fat and nonfat cooking.

Making a Pan Sauce

1 Degrease the pan drippings

If necessary, darken the pan drippings over high heat for 1–2 minutes. Pour the drippings into a fat separator or glass measuring cup and let stand for a few minutes until the fat rises to the top.

2 Replenish the pan juices

Pour the juices from the separator into a glass measuring cup, leaving the fat. (Or, skim the fat from the surface of the juices). Add stock to the degreased pan juices to reach the quantity called for in your recipe.

3 Deglaze the pan

Pour the stock mixture into the pan and bring to a boil, scraping up the browned bits on the bottom and sides of the pan with a wooden spoon. These browned bits will add a rich flavor to the final sauce.

4 Reduce the sauce

Let the sauce boil until it has reduced according to the directions in the recipe. The timing will depend on the quantity of liquid you start with. Tilt the pan to estimate the amount of remaining liquid.

5 Thicken the sauce, if desired

If you desire a thicker sauce, whisk together equal parts cornstarch and water. Whisk a little of the mixture into the simmering sauce, then bring to a boil briefly just until the sauce thickens.

6 Finish the sauce with butter

Remove the pan from the heat. While whisking constantly, drop in a few small butter cubes, 1 or 2 at a time. The sauce will gain a slightly thicker body and nice sheen. Season to taste and use right away.

Dicing an Onion

1 Halve the onion
Using a large chef's knife, cut the onion in half lengthwise right through the root and stem ends. This initial cut makes the onion easier to peel and gives each half a flat side for stability when cutting.

2 Peel the onion
Using a paring knife, and starting at the stem end of each onion half, pick up the edge of the papery skin and pull it away. If the first layer of flesh has rough or papery patches, remove it, too.

3 Trim the onion
Trim each end neatly, leaving some of the root end intact to help hold the onion half together. Place an onion half, flat side down and with the root end facing away from you, on the cutting board.

4 Cut the onion half lengthwise
Hold the onion half securely on either side. Using the chef's knife, make a series of lengthwise cuts, as thick as you want the final dice to be. Do not cut all the way through the root end.

5 Cut the onion half horizontally
Spread your fingers across the onion half to help keep it together. Turn the knife blade parallel to the cutting board and make a series of horizontal cuts as thick as you want the final dice to be.

6 Cut the onion half crosswise
Still holding the half together with your fingers, cut it crosswise into dice. To mince the pieces, rest the fingertips of one hand on the tip of the knife, and rock the blade back and forth over the pieces.

Mincing a Shallot

  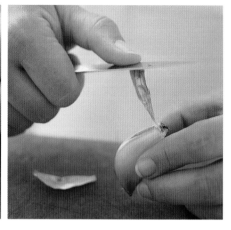

1 Separate the cloves
Sometimes you'll find plump, individual bronze-skinned shallots; other times they resemble garlic heads, with 2 or more cloves attached to one another. Separate the cloves, if necessary.

2 Halve the shallot
When you are first learning to dice shallots, you may want to use a paring knife. As you gain skill, you can switch to a larger knife. Cut the shallot in half lengthwise through the root and stem ends.

3 Peel and trim the shallot
Using the knife, pick up the edge of the shallot's papery bronze skin and pull it away. Trim each end neatly, but leave some of the root intact to help hold the shallot half together as you cut.

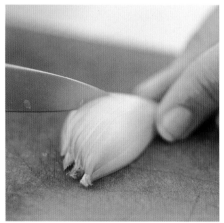  

4 Cut the shallot half lengthwise
Put the flat side of the shallot half on the cutting board and make a series of thin lengthwise cuts. Do not cut all the way through the root end; it will hold the shallot layers together.

5 Cut the shallot half horizontally
Turn the knife blade parallel to the cutting board and make a series of thin horizontal cuts through the shallot half. Stop just short of the shallot's root end to help keep the shallot half together.

6 Cut the shallot half crosswise
Finally, cut the shallot half crosswise to dice. Dicing a shallot in this way yields pieces that will cook evenly. To mince the shallot, rock the knife blade back and forth over the pieces until very finely cut.

Working with Mint, Basil, or Sage

1 Select the herb
Large-leafed herbs such as basil (top left), sage (top right), and mint (bottom) can be either slivered or chopped. Choose bunches with bright green, fragrant leaves. Avoid those with wilted or discolored leaves.

2 Pull the leaves from the stems
Rinse the herbs and spin dry in a salad spinner or pat them dry thoroughly with paper towels. Use your fingers to pull off the large leaves one at a time from the stems. Discard the stems and any discolored leaves.

3 Stack and roll the leaves
Stack 5 or 6 individual herb leaves on top of one another on the cutting board, then roll the stack lengthwise into a tight cylinder. It's best to stack leaves that are approximately the same size.

4 Cut the leaves into ribbons
Using a chef's knife, cut the leaves crosswise into narrow slivers. These ribbons are known by chefs as a chiffonade. To chop the herbs, gather the slivers into a pile and rock the blade over them to cut into small pieces.

HERBS & FLAVORS

The following herbs are used throughout the book, offering fresh, verdant flavor to a variety of dishes.

Basil is sweet and mild, with a faint hint of anise and cloves

Chives boast slender, bright green stems with a fresh, onion-like flavor

Cilantro has a pleasantly biting and lightly citrusy taste

Dill has fresh, feathery leaves with a distinctive grassy aroma

Marjoram is an earthy herb, milder in flavor than its relative oregano

Mint lends a cool, refreshing, "green" flavor to sweet or savory dishes

Oregano is aromatic, pungent, and spicy, used in many savory dishes

Parsley adds vibrant color and pleasing, faintly peppery, fresh flavor

Rosemary has a fragrance evoking musk and woods; use sparingly

Sage has soft, gray-green leaves that are sweet, aromatic, and woodsy

Tarragon is distinctively sweet; its flavor recalls that of anise

Thyme delivers floral, earthy flavor to all types of food

Working with Oregano, Marjoram or Thyme

1 Select the herb
Small-leafed, branched herbs such as thyme (right), marjoram (left), and oregano (top) are a bit hardier than other herbs. Choose bunches with bright green, fragrant leaves. Avoid bundles with limp stems or branches.

2 Remove the leaves
Rinse the herbs and pat them completely dry with paper towels. Remove the petal-like leaves by gently running your thumb and index finger down the stems. Discard the stems and any discolored leaves.

3 Chop the leaves
To chop, gather the leaves on a cutting board. Rest the fingertips of one hand on the tip of a chef's knife and rock the blade back and forth briefly over the leaves to chop coarsely.

4 Finely chop or mince
Continue to regather the leaves and rock the blade back and forth over them until they are chopped into small, even pieces (finely chopped), or into pieces as fine as possible (minced).

Working with Rosemary

1 Remove the leaves
Rinse the rosemary and pat it dry with paper towels. To remove the sturdy leaves of rosemary, carefully run your thumb and index finger down the stems or pull the leaves off the stems with your fingertips.

2 Finely chop or mince
Rest the fingertips of one hand on the tip of a chef's knife and rock the blade back and forth over the leaves. You'll want to finely chop or mince rosemary since it has a strong flavor and sharp leaves.

Working with Tarragon, Parsley, or Cilantro

Snipping Chives

1 Select the herb

Small-leafed herbs such as tarragon (top left), flat-leaf parsley (right), and cilantro (bottom) are delicate. Choose bunches with bright green, fragrant leaves. Avoid those with wilted leaves.

2 Pluck the leaves from the stems

Rinse the herbs and spin dry in a salad spinner or pat dry thoroughly. Grasp the leaves between your thumb and index finger and pluck them from the stems. Discard the stems and any discolored leaves.

1 Gather the chives into a bundle

Discard any wilted or yellowed chives. Rinse the chives and pat them completely dry with paper towels. Gather a small amount of the blades into a little bundle that fits comfortably in your hand.

3 Chop the leaves

Gather the herb leaves in a pile on the cutting board. Rest the fingertips of one hand on the tip of a chef's knife and rock the blade back and forth briefly over the leaves to chop them coarsely.

4 Finely chop or mince the leaves

Continue to regather the leaves and rock the knife blade back and forth over them until they are chopped into small, even pieces (finely chopped), or into pieces as fine as possible (minced).

2 Snip the chives

Using kitchen scissors, finely snip the chives into small pieces or snip them into slightly longer lengths as directed. (Alternatively, use a very sharp chef's knife to cut the chives into slices.)

Using a Chimney Starter

1 Stuff the chimney starter
A chimney starter is an easy way to start a charcoal fire without imparting unwanted flavors to your food. Remove the grill grate. Upend the chimney starter on the fire bed and stuff loosely with newspaper.

2 Add the coals
Remove the cooking grate from the grill and turn the chimney starter right side up on the fire bed, keeping the newspaper secure in the bottom. Add briquettes or hardwood charcoal to the top of the canister.

3 Ignite the newspaper
Using a gas wand or long-handled match, light the newspaper. The flames will rise upward and ignite the coals. Let the coals burn in the chimney starter until covered with a layer of white ash.

TROUBLESHOOTING
If the newspaper is packed too firmly in the chimney, it will hinder the oxygen flow and prevent the paper from lighting. You should only need 2–3 full sheets of crumpled paper. Remove some as needed and restart the fire.

Direct-heat Fire

1 Pour the ignited coals
When the coals in the chimney starter are covered with a layer of white ash, protect your hand and arm with a grill mitt, turn the chimney starter over, and dump the coals into the fire bed.

2 Arrange the coals
Using long-handled tongs, arrange the coals 2–3 layers deep in one-third of the fire bed and 1–2 layers deep in another third, leaving the remaining third free of coals. Move food to the cool part to control flare-ups.

Indirect-heat Fire

1 Arrange the coals on two sides
After pouring the coals into the fire bed (see left), use long-handled tongs to arrange the coals in 2 equal piles on 2 sides of the grill, leaving a wide area in the center of the fire bed free of coals.

2 Position a drip pan
Place an aluminum-foil pan in the area in the center of the coals to catch the dripping fat and create a cool zone for the grill. To control smoke, add enough water to fill the pan halfway up the sides.

Using Wood Chips

1 Soak the wood chips
Soak hardwood chips, such as mesquite, hickory, or cherry, in a large bowl with water to cover. Let soak for at least 30 minutes. The wet chips will smolder on the fire, producing a good head of smoke.

2 Add the wood chips
For a charcoal grill, sprinkle a handful of soaked wood chips directly onto the hot coals. For a gas grill, add the wood chips to a smoker box according to the manufacturer's directions.

Oiling the Grill Grate

1 Dip rolled paper towels in oil
Pour a moderate amount of canola oil into a small container. Fold a stack of 4 paper towels in half, then roll them up tightly into a cylinder. Using tongs, grasp the towel roll and soak them in the oil.

2 Rub the grate with the oil
Still using the tongs, brush the grill grate with the oiled towels. The oil keeps food, particularly fish and other delicate items, from sticking to the grill grate and makes cleanup easier.

Safety & Temperature

Safe handling of raw ingredients is especially important when working with raw poultry, which has some specific concerns. Pay close attention to temperatures to ensure that harmful bacteria are destroyed.

Poultry & Food Safety

All perishable meat, fish, and poultry are subject to contamination by harmful bacteria, and one of these, salmonella, has been particularly linked with raw or undercooked birds.

Keep all poultry as cold as possible before cooking. Cold temperatures inhibit bacterial growth: 40°F (5°C) or slightly below is the optimal temperature. Take poultry home within an hour after purchase and refrigerate immediately in the coldest part of the refrigerator. Use it within 2 days of purchase. Many recipes recommend taking the bird out of the refrigerator briefly to enhance even cooking.

Handling Poultry

Always handle raw poultry carefully to avoid cross-contamination of food preparation surfaces, and never allow it to come into contact with foods that will be eaten raw, such as green salad. There is no need to rinse poultry; it only refreshes the bird, rather than cleans it, and you risk contaminating the sink and counter tops by splashing the rinsing water onto them. Reserve one cutting board for raw poultry, meats, and

seafood and another one for produce, and wash the former thoroughly with hot, soapy water and dry well between uses.

Testing for Doneness

Salmonella is killed at about 160°F (71°C), and a whole chicken is done at 170°F (77°C). To test, insert the thermometer into the thickest part of the thigh without touching bone, which can skew the reading. Or, if you lack a thermometer, check for clear juices by piercing the thigh joint with the tip of a knife.

Visual or textural cues are also used for cuts that are too thin or too small to be tested with a thermometer. For boneless, skinless chicken breast, the center should feel firm and spring back when pressed with a fingertip. And when you stir-fry boneless, skinless chicken pieces, they should be opaque throughout when cut into with a knife.

Keep in mind that food temperature will rise slightly after cooking. This is called carryover cooking, and it should be taken into account when you check the doneness of poultry. The exact increase depends on the size and shape of the food and the cooking temperatures. Pay attention to the cues in the recipes for safe, but still juicy results.

Testing Boneless Poultry Pieces

1 Test by sight
For small pieces of boneless poultry, such as thighs or breast halves, use a paring knife to make a small cut into the meat. When properly cooked, the flesh should be opaque throughout with no sign of pink.

2 Test by touch
For thin pieces of poultry, such as pounded boneless breasts, press the center of the poultry piece with a fingertip. It should feel firm, but bounce back, indicating the poultry is cooked but not overdone.

Testing Bone-In Poultry

1 Test a whole bird
To test a whole bird for doneness, insert an instant-read thermometer into the thickest part of the thigh away from the bone. When the poultry is done, the thermometer should read 170°F (77°C).

2 Test a bone-in cut
To test a large individual cut, such as a turkey breast, insert an instant-read thermometer into the center of the thickest part of the cut, away from the bone. When done, it should read 170°F (77°C).

USING LEFTOVERS

A roasted chicken just out of the oven is delicious, but there are also any number of ways to turn leftover chicken into an equally satisfying dish the next day. Try the Roast Chicken Sandwich (page 97), or the Layered Chicken Enchiladas (page 93), or one of the following ideas.

Curried Chicken Salad
Combine diced chicken, diced celery, golden raisins, mayonnaise, and curry powder to taste. Serve on a bed of red-leaf lettuce.

Cobb Salad
Arrange chicken breast slices on a bed of lettuce leaves with avocado cubes and wedges of tomato and hard-boiled egg. Garnish with crumbled blue cheese and bacon. Drizzle with your favorite dressing.

Savory Chicken Pasta
Cook wide pasta strands until al dente. While the pasta is draining, cut chicken into pieces, and warm it with leftover pan sauce over low heat. Toss with the pasta and serve with grated Parmesan cheese.

Risotto with Chicken & Peas
Prepare your favorite risotto recipe. During the last three minutes of cooking, stir in 2 cups diced roasted chicken meat and 1 cup cooked fresh or frozen peas. Sprinkle with freshly grated Parmesan cheese.

Serving & Garnishing

Preparing delicious food is only part of the joy of cooking. Creating an appealing presentation is the final step in creating a pleasurable meal, whether casual or festive, and no matter what the occasion.

Whole birds and large cuts of poultry are particularly festive and make an attractive centerpiece for any meal, whether casual or formal. If carving a whole bird at the table makes you feel intimidated, present it on a beautiful serving platter, then bring it back to the kitchen to carve. While you are carving the bird, gently warm the serving platter. Arrange the sliced meat on the warmed platter, grouping the white meat and dark meat together to pass at the table. Remember to set out a large serving fork to help guests move the food from the platter to their plates.

When carving or slicing smaller cuts, pay attention to the cues in the recipes, as they will guide you to the best technique for carving or slicing to enhance the flavor and texture of the bird. For example, duck breast should be thinly sliced on the diagonal to make wide, attractive pieces. For any poultry, always look for the "grain" or the direction of the fibers in the flesh, which run in one direction. Carving the meat across the grain cuts it into shorter fibers and makes it easier to eat and more tender.

To keep cooked poultry at an optimal serving temperature, place it on warmed plates or platters. Warm the tableware in an oven at its lowest setting (or a turned-off oven if recently used) for about 10 minutes. Or, set tableware near the stove while roasting or broiling. Make sure to use oven mitts when handling in case it becomes too hot.

Serving typically falls into two camps: family style, a casual approach where the food is arranged on large platters and brought to the table for guests to serve themselves; and restaurant-style, a more formal style where individual dishes are plated in the kitchen and then brought to the table. However, the rules don't need to be rigidly applied. Passing platters at a fancy dinner strikes a welcome note of conviviality. And often, individual plates are easier to put together for serving and welcomed, even for a family meal.

Don't overlook the importance of a garnish: a nicely presented dish tempts both the eye and the palate. Garnishing is all about harmony. Look for attractive ingredients in the recipe—making sure they are always edible—that will make visual accents in the presentation: slices of citrus fruits; fresh herbs, either chopped for individual plates or sprigs on large platter.

Carving a Whole Chicken

1 Expose the thigh joints
Place the bird breast side up on a carving board. Using kitchen scissors, remove the trussing string, if present. Steadying the bird with a carving fork, use a knife to cut through the skin between the breast and the thigh.

2 Remove the legs
Using your other hand, move a leg downward to locate the joint where the thigh meets the body. Cut through the joint to sever the leg. Repeat on the other side of the bird to remove the second leg.

3 Separate the thighs
Holding a leg securely with one hand, cut through the joint between the drumstick and thigh to separate them (it is sometimes easier to find on the underside of the leg). Repeat with the second leg.

4 Remove the wings
Cut through the skin between a wing and the breast. Locate the joint where the wing meets the body and cut through it to remove the wing. Repeat on the other side to remove the second wing.

5 Make a base cut at the breast
The breast meat can be difficult to slice, or the slices can fall apart. Before carving, make a deep horizontal cut through the breast toward the bone, creating a base cut. This way, each slice will end neatly at the base cut.

6 Carve the breasts
Beginning at the breastbone, make a series of cuts downward and parallel to the rib cage, carving the meat from one side of the breast in long, thin slices. Repeat to carve the meat on the other side of the breast.

Basic Recipes

The following pages offer some staple recipes for stocks, sauces, and accompaniments that are called for throughout the book, but which are also useful additions to any cook's repertoire.

Chicken Stock

3 lb (1.5 kg) chicken backs and/or wings, chopped into 2- to 3-inch (5- to 7.5-cm) pieces

2 tbsp canola oil

1 small yellow onion, coarsely chopped

1 small carrot, coarsely chopped

1 small stalk celery with leaves, coarsely chopped

1 cup (8 fl oz/250 ml) water

4 sprigs fresh thyme or ½ teaspoon dried thyme

6 peppercorns

1 small bay leaf

Preheat the oven to 425°F (220°C). Spread the chicken pieces, overlapping slightly if necessary, in a large roasting pan. Roast for 30 minutes. Remove from the oven and, using tongs, turn the chicken pieces. Return to the oven and continue roasting until the chicken pieces are deeply browned, about 20 minutes longer.

Meanwhile, place a 6- to 8-qt (6- to 8-l) stockpot or Dutch oven over medium heat and add the oil. When hot, add the onion, carrot, and celery and cook, stirring occasionally, until the vegetables are beginning to brown, about 6 minutes.

Remove the pot from the heat. Remove the roasting pan from the oven and transfer the browned chicken pieces to the pot. Discard the fat in the roasting pan. Place the roasting pan over 2 burners on the stove top and turn on the heat to high. When the pan drippings begin to sizzle, carefully pour the 1 cup water into the pan. Bring the water to a boil, scraping up the browned bits in the pan. Pour the brown liquid that is created into the pot.

Pour water into the pot just to cover the ingredients and place over high heat. Bring just to a boil, skimming off any foam that rises to the top. Reduce the heat to low, add the thyme, peppercorns, and bay leaf, and simmer, regularly skimming any new foam that rises to the surface, until the stock is full flavored, at least 3 hours or up to 6 hours. As the stock cooks, add hot water if necessary to keep the ingredients submerged, and never allow the stock to come to a boil.

Line a large fine-mesh sieve with damp cheesecloth and place the sieve over a large heatproof bowl. Carefully pour the stock through the sieve into the bowl. Remove the sieve and discard the solids. Let the stock stand for 5 minutes. With a large metal spoon, skim off the clear yellow fat on the surface of the stock. Use the stock immediately, or cool and store it.

Place the bowl of stock in a larger bowl or sink filled with ice water. Let stand, stirring occasionally, until the stock has cooled to tepid. Cover the stock and refrigerate until well chilled, at least 6 hours or up to overnight. Remove from the refrigerator and, using the large metal spoon, scrape off any solidified fat on the surface of the stock and discard it. Re-cover and refrigerate for up to 3 days. Or, reheat the stock just until it is liquid, pour into airtight containers, cool, cover, and freeze for up to 3 months.

MAKES ABOUT 2 QT (2 L)

Tapenade

1 clove garlic

½ cup (2½ oz/75 g) pitted and coarsely chopped Kalamata olives

1 tsp anchovy paste

1 tsp dried herbes de Provence

½ tsp Dijon mustard

⅛ tsp red pepper flakes

1 tbsp extra-virgin olive oil

With a food processor running, drop the garlic clove into the feed tube to chop it. Stop the processor, add the olives, anchovy paste, herbs, mustard, and pepper flakes. Process until the olives are finely chopped. Again with the machine running, drizzle in the olive oil and process to make a paste.

Transfer to a bowl, cover, and let stand for about ½ hour to blend the flavors.

MAKES ABOUT ¾ CUP (6 FL OZ/180 ML)

Pesto

1 clove garlic

1½ cups (1¾ oz/50 g) firmly packed fresh basil leaves

¼ cup (1 oz/30 g) freshly grated Parmesan cheese

2 tbsp pine nuts

2 tbsp chopped fresh flat-leaf parsley

⅛ tsp salt

Pinch of freshly ground pepper

3 tbsp extra-virgin olive oil

With a food processor running, drop the garlic clove into the feed tube to chop it. Stop the processor, add the basil leaves, Parmesan, nuts, parsley, salt, and pepper. Process until the basil is very finely chopped. Again with the machine running, drizzle in the olive oil and process to make a paste.

Transfer to a bowl, cover, and let stand for about ½ hour to blend the flavors.

MAKES ABOUT ¾ CUP (6 FL OZ/180 ML)

Mango Salsa

1 ripe mango, peeled and diced

½ small serrano chile, seeded and minced

3 green onions, including tender green parts, thinly sliced

½ cup loosely packed fresh cilantro leaves, coarsely chopped

2 tbsp diced red bell pepper

1½ tbsp fresh lime juice

Kosher salt

In a glass bowl, combing the mango, chile, green onions, cilantro, bell pepper, lime juice, and ½ teaspoon salt and stir to combine. Cover and refrigerate for at least 30 minutes or up to 1 hour to allow the flavors to marry.

MAKES ABOUT 2 CUPS (16 FL OZ/500 ML)

Fresh Tomato Salsa

1 lb (500 g) ripe tomatoes, seeded and diced

¼ cup (1½ oz/45 g) finely chopped white onion

¼ cup (⅓ oz/10 g) loosely packed chopped fresh cilantro

3 jalapeño chiles, seeded and minced

2 tsp fresh lime juice

Kosher salt

In a bowl, toss together the tomatoes, onion, cilantro, chiles, and lime juice. Season to taste with salt. Cover and let stand for 10–15 minutes to allow the flavors to mingle.

MAKES ABOUT 2 CUPS (16 FL OZ/500 ML)

Guacamole

6 tbsp (2 oz/60 g) finely chopped white onion

2 serrano chiles, seeded and minced

1 clove garlic, minced (optional)

2 ripe Hass avodacos, halved, pitted, and peeled

1 large, ripe tomato, finely chopped

¼ cup (¼ oz/7 g) lightly packed fresh cilantro leaves, finely chopped

1 tbsp fresh lime juice

Kosher salt

In a bowl, mash 4 tablespoons (1½ oz/45 g) of the onion, the chiles, and the garlic, if using, with a fork to form a coarse paste. Add the avocado and mash until well incorporated. Stir in the tomato, cilantro, and lime juice. Season to taste with salt. Let stand for a few minutes before serving.

MAKES ABOUT 2½ CUPS (20 FL OZ/625 ML)

Red Wine Vinaigrette

1 tbsp red wine vinegar

Coarse sea salt

1 tsp Dijon mustard

3 tbsp extra-virgin olive oil

Freshly ground pepper

Put the vinegar and ½ teaspoon salt in a bowl and stir with a fork to dissolve the salt. With the fork, whisk in the mustard. Slowly pour the oil into the vinegar in a thin stream while whisking with the fork. Season with ¼ teaspoon pepper.

MAKES ABOUT 6 TABLESPOONS (3 FL OZ/90 ML)

Index